SONG TITLE SERIES

SLIM DUSTY

JOAN MAGUIRE

Copyright Page

New: Slim Dusty

Author: Joan Maguire

National Library of Australia Cataloguing-in-Publication – Publication entry

Author:	Maguire, Joan.
Title:	Slim Dusty / Joan Maguire.
ISBN:	9780980855135
Series:	Song title series.
Subjects:	Dusty, Slim, 1927-2003
	Country musician—Australia--Biography

Dewey Number: 781.642092

Published with the assistance of Love of Books and is available through the Print on Demand network and www.songtitleseries.com

This book is also available in a large print format and as an E-book.

This short story book was created and written
By Joan Maguire on 20th October 2010 ©
ISBN: 978-0-9808551-3-5

E-book re-written April 2014© and is available through
the providers listed on www.songtitleseries.com
EIBSN: 978-0-9925964-5-3

The large print book was created in April 2015 © and is available
through the same distributors as the normal book and
www.songtitleseries.com
ISBN: 978-0-9943297-0-7

DEDICATION

I would like to dedicate this book and say to thank you to my Earth Angel David and his friends, who inspire and motivate me to achieve things that I never dreamt, were possible.

INTRODUCTION

I started writing the Song Title Series books because I listen to and enjoy many different genres of music and felt that it was a good and unique way of preserving the different artists or bands works. This is the first of the three books I have written to showcase some of Australia's country men and women.

Slim Dusty was and still is a memorable country music artist. Legally I can not use Lyrics or Music because of Copyright but I can use song titles and due to the nature of my books; legally I must place a Reference (exactly as it is down loaded) and Bibliography in the back of the book. I have not attempted to plagiarize or disregard anyone's copyright by the use of the picture and the actual cover picture used was legally obtained at the time by the original publisher of this book and is mentioned in the bibliography.

So by using 1,644 of his song titles (Italicized) as well as some from his family and friends; I have written the short story about young American male, hitch hiking through Australia via the outback.

He is given a lift by *the old Australian Travelling Showman.* Somehow the *Australian Bushman* seems to know what is troubling the young man, *Duncan* and introduces him to people who help him try to understand his past. With this help along the way, *Duncan* begins to unravel his dreams and life in unusual ways.

When reading this "Song Title Series" book, I hope that no disservice has been done to the band as well as their adoring fans who read it, for that was not my intention. As I may have missed a song, an album or a concert within this book I do apologize sincerely. I have created and written this story without the sanctity of Slim Dusty's family and I hope that if they read this they will enjoy it as well.

Well sit back and enjoy the story and don't forget that because of using the original song titles in whole, there are places in the book that I could not change to make it more comprehensible for you the reader. I also acknowledge that some places mentioned in the book are not in their original states or territory.

ACKNOWLEDGEMENTS

I would like to thank my daughters, Jenny and Kylie for their positive but critical input in the first draft of this book and all the help and support that they have given me throughout the Song Title Series books. With taking their input to mind, I have improved the book.

I would also like to thank my son Peter and his family for their support and help in keeping me grounded.

I would like to say a special thank you to my brother Colin and his wife Beth who have given me so much help in authenticating parts of this story.

I would like to thank, Kay and Julie for their patience and understanding whilst teaching me and giving me the skills to present my unique books in the best way possible.

I would also like to thank Patrick and everyone else who has helped me bring this book to life and to you for purchasing it.

OTHER BOOKS IN THE SONG TITLE SERIES

Bon Jovi – Wanted Dead Or Alive
Green Day
AC/DC
Beach Boys
Slim Dusty
Country Women
Five Country Men
Six Crooners
Three Crooners
ABBA
The Rat Pack
Elton John
Classic 50s & 60s Rock 'N' Roll

CONTENTS

LUCKY DAY

Standing under the *gum trees by the roadway*, the hitch hiker turned his head around to see some *lights on the hill* pass that ran out of the *Mount Bukaroo* Mountains that separated the coastal side of the range from the *Plains of Peppimenarti*.

As the vehicle approached, the hitch hiker stepped closer to the edge of the road and stuck out his thumb and the vehicle slowed to a stop right beside him.

"*G'day g'day*, I'm *Johnny Foster, the old time travelling showman* and one of the *Australian bushmen.*" said the driver. "*Me and Matilda*, this *old sunlander van* of mine are going *down the track* to the *end of the Canning Stock route* and then to *Highway One. I'm going back again to Yarrawonga*, down south, for a *family reunion* at Christmas.

You're lucky that I happened to be passing 'cos there ain't a lot of traffic along these roads these days. Hop in and I'll give you a ride down the ways a bit; mind you, we'll most probably run into some *old mates* of mine further *down the track*.

You look like *an independent bloke*, what's your name?"

"*Duncan.*" said the hitch hiker as he got into the van.

"Well *Duncan*, I think this is your lucky day and you don't sound like a dinki di Aussie. Where you from?" said Johnny.

"No. I'm not from here. I'm a *Louisiana man*. I flew out of *L.A.International Airport*, ten months ago and have been enjoying your *country way of life. Country livin'* here is so different from back home. Here it's a *hard, hard country* where the *dry weather wind* blows everyday, but the people are so friendly.

I am hoping to see *every little bit of Australia* before I have to leave, unless I can change the *beat of the Government stroke* and they let me stay and work here in *Australia*.

Yes, I sure was lucky that you stopped as I don't think that I would have been able to *walk a country mile* today." said *Duncan*.

"What's brought you way out here? I mean, usually overseas travellers stay in the big smoke, the *neon city*, like the *streets of Sydney* or they travel north to the gulf country in the *Queensland State so fair* and warm.

2

They spend a week up there, then fly *from the gulf to Adelaide*, stay there a week then head to *Port Augusta* to catch the *Indian Pacific* to Perth in Western Australia.

After *steppin' round Australia* on the outside so quickly, and sometimes going *fruit pickin' and singin'* while they work, the visitors never get the real *spirit of Australia* like they would if they were to visit places like *The Birdsville Track, Charleville*, the *Snowy River* or visiting a cattle station on the *Plains of Peppimenarti*.

One place I like to visit when I'm travelling is *Joe Maguire's pub* in Tamworth, which is not *a pub with no beer*, especially at the end of January, because many of the *Balladeers of Australia, Bush Poets of Australia* and usually a *singer from down under* will perform there.

Twice daily, a different balladeer might sing the *Ballad of Henry Lawson* or the *Ballad of Port Macquarie* or even the *Ballad of a Drover*; my favourite. A different bush poet might recite the *Bible of the Bush*, a piece by *Henry Lawson* or the story of *the Man from the Never Never*. Some of the singers sing songs like *A Song for Granny*, the *Honky Tonk Blues* or the *Mareeba's Rodeo Song*.

They have a good old *country revival* every year and people will go there from places like *a town like Alice* Springs or from the *Isa* after the *Isa Rodeo* has finished. Mt Isa is a nice place way inland from here.

Charley Gray's Barn dance is the place to be in the evenings to hear the *good old country style fiddler man. I love to have a dance with Dorothy*, who is Charley's wife.

If you ever get the chance to go there, you will hear people asking "Are you *goin' to the barn dance tonight?"* said Johnny.

"Back at *Callaghan's Hotel* in *Camooweal*, the *camp cooks* from the *Keeroongooloo Station* mentioned something about *Kelly's Country Kitchen* and an *old bush barbeque* that they had at Charley's last year but I thought that they were just *campfire yarns* because Tamworth is quite a big town. Isn't it?" said *Duncan*.

"Yes, in fact it's known as the City of Tamworth... Ah! There's the *brass well*, you feeling hungry 'cos the *Three Rivers Hotel* is just ahead and it is not *a pub with no beer*, in fact, wait till you see the sign he has out front.

Sweeny has *so many ballads to play* on his *Regal Zonophone* and his beer is always cold, but mind he doesn't give you a glass of *Finney's home brew* first as it will knock your sox off; it's strong stuff.

He cooks the best steak in these parts and always buys his beef from *Peter Anderson & Co.* who grazes their cattle on the *Plains of Peppimenarti.*" said Johnny.

As they pulled into the dusty car park, *Duncan* saw a sign "THIS IS THE PUB WITH NO BEER" but the word NO was crossed out.

"Two coldies, *Sweeny.*" said Johnny as he walked through the door with *Duncan* close behind him.

"*G'day blue*, haven't see you round these parts for awhile. Where you been; *waltzing Matilda* down the highways and *catching yellowbelly in the old Barcoo* again?" asked Sweeny "and who's the young whipper snapper with you?"

"This is *Duncan*. He's a *man on the side of the road*, standing under some *gum trees by the roadway* hitch hiking, that I picked up and it's a good thing I did 'cos he was *heading for that brumby trail* and the *Range of Glory* where that kid got lost a few years back." said Johnny.

As *Duncan* walked into the hotel, it reminded him of one of the *old time country halls* from back home.

There was a long bar with stools along the front of it, to the left as you walked in through the door; there was a large mirror mounted on the wall that reflected a painting of *The Man from Snowy River*, surrounded by some *cattlemen from the high plains*. Some men were mounted on their *stock horses* on either side of some men who were standing in front of what seemed to be *the grandest homestead of all* with the *blue hills in the distance.*

Underneath the painting was a piano next to a dance floor and opposite the front door next to the bar was another door that led to a dining room, where families could be together and near to that doorway was a big old fashioned open fireplace that warmed the whole place.

On the bar were the heady beers that Johnny had ordered and when they sat down Johnny said "*You've got to drink the froth to get to the beer.*

4

There was a bit of a commotion outside and a voice was heard saying *"How will I go with him, mate?"*

"You'll be OK, just *leave him in the long yard."* was the reply. "C'mon boys, let's get inside of this supposedly *a pub with no beer* and wash the dust from our throats; he'll catch up soon enough."

Sweeny looked at Johnny and said "It's the *cattlemen from the high plains*, the *Cobb and Co. Twitch* Station mob."

The doors burst open and in walked about ten hot and sweaty looking men, who headed straight for the beers that *Sweeny* had already pulled for them.

"G'day Johnny. Knew you were here by the van parked at the *end of the pub*. You been up *catching yellowbelly in the Barcoo* again. I hope you didn't have *a bad day's fishing* with *mad Joe the fisherman*.

Hey *Sweeny*, can I have a pouch of *Auctioneer?"* said one of the boys who then turned to *Duncan* and said *"I must have good terbaccy when I smoke."*

Johnny made the *introduction*, then said *"Things are not the same on the land* theses days, what with the *drought* one day and then *when the rain tumbles down in July*, anything can happen depending on how much rain we get; remember *the flood of '95."*

"Strewth, you're not wrong there mate; us boys have been *mustering in full swing*. We're coming back from *Eumerelle Shore* Station where we delivered *three hundred horses*. We watched as *Middleton's rouseabout* Hank work with *Harry the breaker* who started sorting and working on them.

The floods are just as bad as the drought 'cos it takes the top soil away and as for *Water – if it took fifty years* of continuous steady rain, we still wouldn't have enough. Oh, I don't mean rain every day, but more regular than what we get now. *The rain still tumbles down in July* but it is usually along the coast and not much reaches us out here." said Kelly.

Kelly's offsider said "Hey *Sweeny*, when are you going to take down that sign of yours? *A pub with no beer* won't make people *travellin' through* these parts want to stop here."

Sweeny said "You would be surprised at how many people do stop here because of that sign, especially since I crossed the NO out. They come in here laughing over it. It's a good way to get rid of their *highway blues.*"

Kelly said "You mind if we camp out back for the night. We'll be gone by the *break o' day* 'cos we've gotta get to *Camooweal* in the next couple of days to help with the *drovin'* of *fifteen hundred head* of cattle to the *Plains of Peppimenarti* for *Peter Anderson and Co.* It will be like the *nineteen eighties bushmen on the move* again. At least we're doing it now, not *when the rain tumbles down in July* and the *winter winds* blow cold across the land.

Speaking of which, can we get some of your steaks and snags for the barbie out back and add a carton of your brown bottles as well. Don't worry, we'll cook and *clean up our own backyard* spot when we're finished.

Johnny, do you and *Duncan* wanna join us?

The boys can ride off the *brown bottle blues* tomorrow while they try to figure out the answer to *the pub with no beer.*"

That evening, *Duncan* heard a lot of tales from the drovers; some were about *riding through the valley in spring* to get to *the Blue Gum Tree ball* but he was most interested in the *Ghosts of the Golden Mile* and the *Ghost of Ben Hall*, who was a *nature's gentleman.*

THE REASON

"Mornin' cobber, how did you sleep? The old van's comfy, isn't it? I've been thinking; how'd you like to travel with me a bit? I sure could do with some company for awhile while *ridin' this road* and it beats trying to *walk a country mile* out here in the heat of the *never never*." asked Johnny.

"Sure, that would be great, thanks. I won't get as far each day if I did have to *walk a country mile* continuously everyday. You're the answer to a *traveller's prayer*." said Duncan.

"Well, let's go get ourselves some *ham and eggs* for breakfast and say bye to Sweeny. Before we go too far down the road in the van, I'm gonna have to *fill 'er up*." said Johnny.

It wasn't long before they were *just rollin' on the road to anywhere* or one that would take them south.

"Well, there's *only the two of us here*, so after hearing you saying some stuff last night to a couple of the drovers, do you want to tell me about home and why you'd prefer to stay in Aussie instead of going back home to the States?" enquired Johnny.

Duncan looked out the side window and said quietly, "*My dad was a roadtrain man* who drove an *old Kentucky rig*. I guess that he must have been *born a travellin' man* 'cos he was never home a lot. Mom did the best she could without him being there but I guess *it takes an Irish heart* and a strong will to put up with what she had to put up with.

When dad *finally made it home*, he would bring some of his *old mates* with him and *they drank and drank and drank*; yes, he became known as *the drunkard* of the town and a *no good truckin' man*.

The last time he was home, he was drinking and playing what he called "*the hangover song*" and he sent my *mother* out to get something from the driver's door compartment of his rig.

There she found some *old love letters*; one containing a photo of a young woman sitting on the *banks of the Ohio* River and on the back was written "Yours always, *Cinderella*." and written on the back of another letter was your "Utah love *Clara Waters*."

7

My mother was upset when she went back inside the house and she confronted my dad about the *old love letters*.

My mom had just finished *baking a brownie* cake when she said "*Good Heavens above, do you think that I don't know* when you've been *foolin' around. I don't sleep at night* and sometimes *I fall to pieces* thinking about what would happen *if you fall out of love with me*. It's *no good baby*; I thought that *just lovin' you* was enough to keep bringing you, my *high, wide and handsome* guy, and that *old Kentucky rig* home to us."

Something snapped inside dad and as he lunged to grab mum he said "*I don't want no woman around* me nor any kids either, *I need to find a place* where I can have some peace."

Mum screamed "*Stay away from me, I ain't a-gonna be treated this-a-way* and *if you walk out that gate*, don't come back."

I can still hear dad swearing as he slammed the front door and taking off in his rig, *leaving only dust* in the street.

Memories and dreams still come and go especially when I hear the type of music *my dad played to me* when I was younger.

We moved out of our home and went to live with my grandparents in a different state. *Grandfather Johnson* told my *mother* that *she'll be right* and *he don't deserve you anymore*; she always was her *daddy's girl*, and now both of you have *gotta keep moving* forward.

Everyone seemed to be *crying on each other's shoulder* and I ended up *in my grandmother's arms* as she took me outside to calm me down.

Gran said to me "*Do you think I do not know* what you are going through. My father was an *interstater*. That's right, *my dad was a roadtrain man* as well, but the *roaring wheels* that kept him *roaring through the night* and *rolling down the road* was his downfall.

Under the spell of Highway one, the *whiskey blues*, the *white line* fever and the *lights on the hill* saw us *diggin' a hole* to bury him in. *The biggest disappointment* that I have is that he isn't here to see you or your *mother*.

I knew your father real well and *he's a good bloke when he's sober* but he knows that there's *not much to show* for the years he's been driving."

We went back inside and I told my mum that *I've been talking to grannie* who suggested that I go stay with her *city brother* until you get yourself back on your feet without having to worry about me but *if I needed you*, I'll come back.

Six months later I received *a letter from Arrabury* Lawyers saying that *my old Kentucky home* was up for sale. Although *sadness and I wander home* to my uncle's place each day in the city, *the day I went back home*, to my real home, was *the day we sold the farm* and the day my mother passed away from having a heart attack.

When they gave me my *mother's wedding band*, I went *crazy* and became an *easy going drifter* and ended up over here *bumming around* because I didn't want people *feeling sorry for me* back home in the States. I also thought that I could get over *my faded dream* of working on the land."

"Gee, mate that's tough. No wonder you don't want to go back home, so I guess that *we'll have to stick together* until we can find a way to change the *beat of the Government stroke* and get them to let you stay.

The next *Election Day* is in a few weeks, so maybe a new Government might be easier to try and work things out with. I know a few people in Parliament that we can talk to, but I'm not promising anything. OK.

The *Red Roo Roadhouse* is a few miles ahead so we'll stop there for a bit." said Johnny.

As Johnny and Duncan walked into the Red Roo Roadhouse, a truck driver was leaving and as he was halfway out the door, he turned and said *"Give my regards to Edna.* I got to get to *Charleville* by tomorrow morning."

"G'day, G'day. You're a bit late coming back from *catching yellowbelly in the old Barcoo* this year Johnny." said the man behind the counter.

As he approached a large group of men sitting around many re-arranged tables, Johnny made the *introduction* of the men to Duncan, then turned and said "G'day *Happy Jack.* Nah, I'm *dead on time*, I'm still *waltzing Matilda* the same way as I usually do.

What's happened since the last time I was around here *Happy Jack?"*

9

"*Kelly's offsider* was passing through about a week back and while he was day *dreamin' on the slip rail* out back, he was surprised when this roo came at him and he ended up having a *scrap with a buck kangaroo*. He was a mess when he came in here and told us about it.

Bold Tommy Payne, the cunnin' roo shooter, took off after it but it got in amongst the *stock horses*, so he decided to *leave him in the long yard* rather than stir up the horses.

Tommy was on his way *back to Croajingalong* after delivering his hides to *Camooweal*. He told us that while he was in *Camooweal*, he saw this special doco on T.V.; it was about the *introduction and space shuttle broadcast 1981*.

He also told us that *Australia's on* the *wallaby* now. *The boxing kangaroo, Matilda no more* will grace our country overseas and that they're talking about changing our *Song of Australia* to something else; maybe they'll call it *Waltzing Matilda*, after your van."

"Well, *tie me kangaroo down sport*, the officials can't just dump our Commonwealth Games mascot, it's un-Australian. So *Australia's on the wallaby* now. Is that because of our rugby team is winning all the time?" said Johnny.

He turned to *Billy Mac* and said "You married yet?"

Billy Mac replied "Yeah, *I'm married to my Bulldog Mac. Our wedding waltz* was a trip *from the gulf to Adelaide*, now we're on our honeymoon to the *top of the world, Darwin big heart of the north* and then we're across the top end with a delivery, but instead of one night, I'll have to spend *another night in Broome*.

I feel like one of those *mechanized swaggies* trying to see *every little bit of Australia*, and I have to carry *42 tyres* as spares on this trip but *it's worth it* as the money's good."

A roar of laughter went out from the others after Billy Mac had finished answering.

Their conversation was interrupted by "*I hope they fight again.*"

"Who?" said one of the men.

"*Frankie and Johnny, I hope they fight again.*"

10

"Who?" said another.

"You know, the *King of Kalgoorlie, Frankie and Johnny, King Bundawaal, I hope they fight again*. I had *the front row* seat at the fight when I went down for *the Melbourne Cup* last year.

The number of *old riders in the grandstand* at *the Melbourne Cup* is a lot fewer than *the old riders in the grandstand* who watch the races at *The Birdsville Track*.

I ran into a *ringer from the top end* at the races and we were both glad to be saying *goodbye Melbourne town* the following morning.

He told me his name was *Jim* and then he said "Give me *my Clinch Mountain home* anytime. *That old bush shanty of mine* is *heaven country style*, even *when the rain tumbles down in July* on the *pastures of home*.

The biggest disappointment here is I can't get the terbaccy here that I usually smoke. *I must have good terbaccy when I smoke*. On top of all that, my *Grandfather Johnson* and I had to stay in *a pub with no beer*.

Yes, it really was *a pub with no beer*. There's a few of them down there but *the pubs still make a quid*. I think it's from the *quicksilver* and *a certain kind of gold* that those people put through those pokie machines and some of those people are as *game as Ned Kelly* while they are playing them.

The nature of man is different down there, as making money is what's important to most of them. Country folks enjoy *the land of lots of time* and space."

"Hey Johnny, Where did you meet the young lad?" asked one of the drivers.

"Picked him up, back down the track. He was standing under some *gum trees by the roadway* and must have seen my *lights on the hill* as I was coming down *Mount Bukaroo*.

He was heading away from *Callaghan's Hotel* in *Camooweal* towards the *Three Rivers Hotel*, so I stopped and he's been with me since. He may be young but he's good company and I couldn't let him *walk a country mile* way out here knowing that the *Brass Well* is dry. *It takes a drought*, a long one for *the Brass Well* to dry up.

11

I'm going back again to Yarrawonga for Christmas.

I don't know what Duncan's gonna do yet, I'll have to have *a word to Texas Jack* before he makes up his mind." said Johnny.

One of the drivers got up to leave and said "Catch you again *Happy Jack* and *give my regards to Edna. My old Midnight Special and me* have to be at the *Three Rivers Hotel* to pick up a special load for a property somewhere on the *Plains of Peppimenarti.*"

He turned back to the table and said "You didn't tell us who won the fight or the cup."

"Frankie won the fight, *Althea* the *Boomaroo flyer* won the cup."

FRIENDS

"Right." said Johnny, "We've had a couple of hours rest, so let's hit the road again and see if we can make the town of *Jambalaya* before *sundown*. See you guys again some time, take care."

After they had filled the van with petrol and were well on their way, Johnny said "You've been a quiet fella and you look like you've got the *Aussie doghouse blues*. Wanna tell me what's wrong?"

Duncan said "I take notice of the *things I see around me* and I listen to what people say. Sometimes I wonder if they are a *truthful fella* or are they giving me some *bullock dung narration*. *Grandfather Johnson* told me once that *your best pal is mother* and *you don't know how sad I* feel knowing that she is no longer here to help *take my worries* away and to help me to prepare for *taking on what's next* in my life.

I used to wake up with that *Oh lonesome me* attitude and I have *not much to show* for what I've done with my life up to now. Sometimes I wish that if only I had a *home sweet home* to go to and a *maple sugar sweetheart* waiting there for me, then my *family of man*, and wife would be nearly complete and *showers of blessings* would rain on me if I had a child.

Truckin's in my blood and I didn't know if I wanted to go down that path but after listening to the other drivers, I'm beginning to like the idea but I still don't want to go back home, but I don't want to be *steppin' round Australia* forever either."

"*She'll be right, mate. Some things a man can't fight* and *life is like a river*, it twists and turns; it rushes along sometimes and meanders along at other times. If it builds up too much, like behind a dam, it soon overflows like a waterfall but it only stops if it reaches the sea or dies; like dries up.

Jambalaya is a strange town, a very old place where us white folk live well with the indigenous people. If *the old Jimmy Woodser* is around and starts talking, listen closely to what he has to say; it may help you.

This is *a land he calls his own* and all the *Australian Bushmen* have respect for him and they enjoy listening to him.

Why worry now about anything that's out of your control at present?"

Duncan nodded off for awhile until a sudden bump in the road aroused him, as they were passing *Bunda Waterhole*, near the inaccessible *Nulla Creek*. It was also where *the old bullock dray* teams would stop with a *whoa, bullocks whoa*, while travelling in the *wagon trains north, up the old Nulla road*.

As they drove *along the road to Nulla Nulla*, and crossed over the dry *Nulla Creek* Johnny said "It ain't like this *when the rain tumbles down in July* and then they turned left into an *old bush road* and followed it until they stopped in front of a *little old one horse pub*, a real *old bush pub* that was built on a bit of a rise.

"We'll stop here for a drink before we hit Jambalaya, ten minutes down the road. There's not a pub in the town, only a motel. This place was built a long time ago for the Jackaroo to rest at because *the saddle is his home* for many weeks of the year." said Johnny.

As they walked towards the pub they heard "There's *no place on earth like Australia.*"

They turned to see an *old feller* sitting by an *old Gidgee tree* and an *old dingo* lying stretched out behind him.

The men from the Nulla Nulla tribe and the *Jimberella kid* were standing *by a fire of Gidgee coal*, dressed and decorated for some sort of tribal dancing.

Then from behind they heard "Johnny, *it's good to see you mate*. You been up *catching yellowbelly in the Barcoo* again?"

They turned back to see an indigenous young man walking towards them.

"*Inigo Jones-Indigo Jones*, yes, *I'm going back again to Yarrawonga* for Christmas. How have you been and whatcha been up to?" asked Johnny.

"I've just come back from the *Innamincka muster* and now we're *back with the show again* while it travels these parts. In about half an hour, we're going to practice our *Corroboree sequence* and *the old Jimmy Woodser*, is going to tell one of his *dream time* stories.

You know that he's one of the *last of the breed* of elders who still tells old stories.

Go, wash the dust from your throats and come back out and join us.

You both will be quite welcome to watch and listen. I am not in this dance bit but I usually translate the story as he speaks it 'cos he does it in many different lingos, however today he will tell the story in your lingo." said Indigo.

As they walked *side by side* into the pub, *old Gilbert* looked up and said "The usual?"

They finished a couple of beers and went outside to join the others *by the fire of Gidgee coal.*

Jimmy Woodser began "More than *a thousand years ago, a little boy called Smiley* and a *little girl dressed in blue, a girl from the land,* walked across this earth and when they spoke, it was in *dream time voices.* They told us *"Don't laugh in the face of father time* because he is the one who controls the *drought time* and says when *the big wet is over."*

Then they talked about *the frog, big frogs in little puddles* trying to work out the *canetoad's plain code.* They also said that *Captain Thunderbolt* will stop them when the *blackened quarts are boiling* and the *Ghosts of the Golden Mile* will stop them as well because *your country's been sold* by the *foolscap tombstones* in the big city."

Then Jimmy looked Duncan in the eyes and said *"There's a rainbow over the rock* and *there's a rainbow around my memories* and yours. You and I have *too many memories too forget* and that *the ace of hearts* will not let *old love letters* hurt you anymore. You do not have as many memories as me so *now is the hour* for you to start changing them. *Itching feet, ramblin' shoes* and *many yesterday's ago* will only leave you in *no man's land.*

It is time for us all to go to our nights *resting place* and become a *dreamer,* for *the Angel of Goulburn Hill* is flying this night *when the moon across the bushland beams* and will stop your *night watch blues."*

Duncan asked Johnny if he knew what Jimmy meant and all Johnny would say was "Sleep on it tonight and we'll talk tomorrow when we're on the road."

At the *break o' day,* Johnny and Duncan were *sittin' on the old front veranda* at *the round table* waiting for their breakfast to be served at the

15

motel when Duncan remarked "This really is *the pub that doesn't sell beer*, isn't it?"

Johnny sat quietly for awhile, staring out to *where the desert flowers bloom* in the early morning and listening to the background music of a *Slim Dusty recording* being played on an old *wind up gramophone*, then said "Yes, this is, and there are a few more around, mind you, *the pubs still make a quid. When the rain tumbles down in July*, some places get a lot of rain but others don't get any.

One year, *somewhere up in Queensland*, near the gulf country, an unexpected long rain period caused many of the *big gulf rivers* to flood and on their journeys south, the rivers flooded places like *Camooweal, Charleville, Eumerella Shores* Station and even *the Birdsville Track*.

A *Middleton's rouseabout* heard of the coming flood from *Sally – the girl on Channel 8* and took off to the stables shouting "*Just saddle old Darkie* for me. I have to try and reach the *cattlemen from the high plains* who are diving *three hundred horses* towards the *Three Rivers Hotel* and warn them before the flood waters get them."

He reached them in time but on his way back to the station, a *bushwacker* took old Darkie and left the *Middleton's rouseabout* tied to a post amongst the *gumtrees by the roadway*.

This place went under and like all flooded places, supplies were unavailable. It started off as *a pub with no beer* but sold spirits and wine, and when they ran out, the owner gave up and sold up as it was not the first time he had been flooded out and again was a substantial financial loss for him to try and recover from. *I wonder if the creeks are still flowing* up north.

Since then the new owners have made it into an overnight motel for travellers. Ah, brekkie. Dig in and then we'll hit the road again."

They had been on the road for about half an hour, when Johnny brought up the subject of Jimmy Woodser's story. "What thoughts have you had about it?"

Duncan said "There was a lot I didn't understand; like the frogs, the foolscap tombstones and the blackened quarts are boiling but I was surprised when he mentioned the rainbow around my memories and old love letters.

16

I thought about it last night in bed and a conclusion that I came up with is; that if I keep dwelling on the past hurts I have had and if I keep moving from place to place, like I'm trying to run away from them, then I'll always be running.

If I start now to try and accept what has happened in my past, then I can make a new future for myself. As for this spirit of the earth – earth angel, David, well, that seems to be just as he said it, a dream time story from way back when and I won't be *losin' my blues tonight* over them."

"Don't ignore *what the man said* about the dream time stories. It is considered *big time*, if the story told by them is meant for you. *That's the kind of religion for me*, the indigenous people believe in it so don't knock them if you don't know or believe in them or the teller's customs.

We've done us proud so far, living off the land and listening to people who know what they are talking about, our past generations of family and friends." said Johnny.

He then continued by saying "When Jimmy spoke about the frogs in little puddles, the canetoad codes and the foolscap tombstones, he was talking about the pollies over the decades and how they have tried to do the right thing for the country; however, all they seemed to do is keep selling bits and pieces of our industries to overseas buyers and one day in the future our country won't belong to us anymore.

The bush has had enough with the mining companies always trying to find a new place to drill and *it takes a drought* not *wagon trains north* to tell us *when the harvest days are over*. The country will be in big trouble when that does happen 'cos not only will we lose the grains; we will also lose the vegies and fruit trees, cattle and sheep. Even if *the rain still tumbles down*, it will not be enough to supply all the land with enough water for crops and live stock.

Cunnamulla is a couple of hours drive and I wasn't gonna stop, but I think you should visit a place there. *The bloke who serves the beer* at the place we'll stay at is a *Cunnamulla fella*.

The countryside between here and there is still just *as Leichhardt saw it then,* when he passed this way many years ago."

As they were travelling, Duncan looked out at the monotonous scenery going by and he thought of and realized a few unusual things.

17

Since he had been picked up by Johnny, who just happened to be passing at the time he was unable to *walk a country mile* much further, they had never passed another vehicle on the road, going in either direction.

Johnny hasn't told him anything about himself, only where he was heading to and he talks and acts like one of the old *Australian Bushmen* but he hasn't got *hard and calloused hands* like you would expect him to have.

This chap knows a lot more than he is letting on, because he has an uncanny way of knowing what I'm thinking and feeling at a certain time, and he seems to introduce me to the right people and the feeling I get from him, is, as if he's *like a family to me* and not a stranger."

His thoughts were broken when Johnny looked and smiled at him as if he knew what he had been thinking, then said "Cunnamulla is just five clicks up the road. This town is a major cross road for you.

In the morning, I'm going to continue on down south; you can come with me or go your own way. It's up to you?"

TURNING POINT

They drove through the town, before pulling into the car park of the *Belt & Buckled* Hotel/Motel.

Duncan looked around the car park and towards the *blue hills in the distance*; the view reminded him of *a picture of home* except for the *gumtrees by the roadway* and *the Johnsonville dance* sign.

"G'day G'day." said Johnny as he walked through the front door of the hotel, "I'd like to book a couple of rooms for the night in the motel section if you have any empty."

"G'day Blue." said *Bill*, who then looked at Duncan standing behind Johnny, "Coming back from *catching yellowbelly in the old Barcoo?"*

"Yeah." said Johnny "I was going to head straight through to Tamworth but Duncan here needs some time to figure out what he's gonna do, so I thought that this would be a good place to stop. Not too many places ahead before Tamworth."

Johnny tossed Duncan a room key and said "Go clean up and rest a bit. I'll meet you in the bar in an hour."

Johnny turned back to *Bill* and asked "Is *Banjo* or *Bonner* still around these parts, I need to talk to one of them about an important matter?"

"Hang on; I'll just go see if *Banjo's man* is still here." replied Bill as he disappeared into another room.

"Johnny, this is *Logan, Banjo's man*. He will take you out to Banjo who is helping to fix the *lights on the hill*. Some folks knocked them crooked during their party last night." said Bill.

"Must've been a hell of a party" for them to be able to do that." said Johnny.

As they were driving out in the old Holden Ute to where Banjo was, Johnny inquire "Are you a *Cunnamulla fella* or are you from somewhere else and how long have you been *Banjo's man?"*

"I've been *Banjo's man* for nearly two years now.

He needed some help when he was working on a *truckie's last will and testament* and because I'm a local, I was able to give him the help he needed. Banjo had *a word to Texas Jack* and I spent two months in *Charleville* and four months in *Camooweal* training for this job.

Both Banjo and Texas Jack are good blokes to work for.

Bonner works away in the bush a lot so we don't get to see him much. There's Banjo now. It looks like he's finished fixing the *lights on the hill.*" said *Logan.*

It was nearly an hour and a half before Johnny joined Duncan at the bar.

"Now, first things first." said Johnny "I'm gonna have a *good old feed of flathead* and a schooner of Four X, then there's somewhere I want to take you and some people I want you to meet. It'll only take a couple of hours, after that you'll be on your own as I have to attend to some other business while I'm here.

Let me know in the morning what you wanna do; go your own way or continue on with me, either way, the choice is yours."

Within the hour, both Johnny and Duncan were standing on *Calvary Hill* and saw *two old gentlemen* sitting at a picnic table under what seemed to be *the world's biggest Cedar tree*, motioning for them to come and join them.

As Johnny and Duncan sat down opposite the other two men, one of them pulled a six pack out of their small esky and said "*We're just a couple of boys from the bush* but *Dick Drumduff* and me come up here each week and have a beer with *the boys who never returned* from the wars." said Ivenhoe.

Then Dick said "*Old Ivenhoe* and I are the last *two Rats of Tobruk*, living in these parts. I remember the day we were shipped out from Townsville; in *beautiful Queensland* on what was once a *luxury liner* with many other young men. *Many mothers* were there to wave us off and as we headed out to sea, the *lights on the hill* behind Townsville shone brightly *and the band played Waltzing Matilda.*

Our ship rendezvoused with other ships near Perth, where soldiers who had come across the Nullarbor Plains on the *Indian Pacific* train, joined the convoy as we sailed for Africa and war.

20

Ivenhoe and I were assigned to C Company, where many country boys were stationed. You could always tell the *Australian Bushmen* from the others, by their *dinkum bushman's hands* and how they could *walk a country mile* in the rough terrain over there that was like the *sands of Tamin* desert here in Aussie.

It was definitely not a fit place to wear *lace up shoes*, sometimes, especially *when the rain tumbles down in July*, you had trouble keeping your army boots on and they became *boots of many colour*, texture and weight.

At night, some of us would sit around and have a *campfire yarn* or two, maybe even without the fire, and if it was safe enough, we would have our style of *country revival* by singing songs like *Waltzing Matilda* and *Click Goes The Shears*, but *when Snowy sings of home*, the *song for the Aussie*, the *singer from down under*, sounded like *God's own singer of songs* and he made you think of home.

I remember one *Christmas, when I was as big as you*, Captain *Kelly's offsider*, Private *Henry Lawson* brought us some *letters from down under* and we were each given a letter to read. I didn't recognize the writing on the envelope and when I opened it and it started with *To Whom It May Concern*, I got worried until I started reading the rest of the letter.

A young female school teacher, who we called *the angel of Goulburn Hill* had gotten each of her pupils to write a letter to a soldier fighting overseas and then arranged for the army to distribute them. Before long, *the spirit of Australia* saw many more letters arrive for the boys, and they would *keep the homefires burning* and *keep the lovelight shining* for *my Aussie home*.

Later that day, the enemy hit us with everything they had, we *copped the lot*. Many men were injured and killed. I found Private *Henry Lawson's pen* as I went to help a *dying stockman* from *Keeroongooloo Station*. His last words were *"You can't take Australia from me* so tell her; *you made me live, love and die* for you. *It's a long way to Tipperarry* but I don't think that I'll make it that far."

The *Abalinga mail* run was on a *lonesome road of tears* as it brought the sad news to families. *Somebody's mother tonight* will still be grieving for the loved one who caught the *Glory Bound train* home. *Do you think that I do not know* how hard it was for all those young men, who now sit here as *names upon the wall* and how each man died *a prouder man than you* or I will ever be?"

21

Ivenhoe put his empty tinnie to one side, and then said "It was in that skirmish that I copped one in the leg and was shipped home. An enemy sub torpedoed one of our hospital ships sending all on board into the *dark depths of the blue* ocean; leaving no survivors. I was sent *back to my old northern home* to have *Christmas on the station* with my folks.

I was then sent with a detachment of Diggers to New Guinea, the *land of no second chance*, the *Kokoda Track, a hard hard country* to trek through. And the enemy, well, compared to them, *Ned Kelly was a gentleman* and they were *as game as Ned Kelly* to some degree but *Harry and the breaker*, the code breaker, soon had the tides turning in our favour.

There was no time for *crying on each others shoulders* when times were rough and it was tough *getting up and goin' Sonny* but we Diggers did just that; we pushed the enemy back to where they came from with the help of the Americans who were waiting on the other side of the island. The death and injury toll was very heavy from our men, from the *men who came behind* us and from the *men who come behind* them.

The *girl I left behind* became an army nurse but was stationed in Australia. *She wasn't there to meet me* when I got home and I found out that *Casey's luck* had run out when Darwin was bombed by the Japanese and her sleeping quarters suffered a direct hit.

Except for Dick, *all my mates are gone* to *the grandest homestead of all*, where *God will prevail* and *Jesus takes a hold* of *my heaven on earth, my home on the sunburnt plains.*

We have both been *from here to there and back* again and *from there to now*, we have seen *the soldier's wife* grieve for her husband who was on *the ship that never returned* and has made a new life. *The things I see around me* in *this country of mine* are changing. *Things are not the same on the land* anymore nor are they anywhere else in the world.

And *about this hat, a brown slouch hat* was once worn with pride but not so much anymore.

The *footsteps coming home* from our heroes with their *names upon the wall* are not being heard so much by the kids of your generation. *Sadness and I wandered home* with *my pal alcohol* after the war and I am one of *the men who try and try* again to *pick it up and pass it on* to the new generation, about the destruction and waste of human life and resources in the event of un-needed wars.

Our memories and our fight is the *closest thing to freedom* that we could ever give someone else. *A rose of red* is a *rose of rememberance* and love. It was *written afterwards* that *we've done us proud*, to go and fight for our freedom and the world's freedom."

Then Johnny said to Duncan "I know that you're not from here and their stories may not mean much to you, but the same sort of men fought and died for your country, so that you can make your own choices in life.

You can either be a '*second class, wait here*' sort of person or you can do something with your life. *Some things a man can't fight* no matter how hard he tries, but you are in control of your own life when you become an adult.

You told me many things about yourself and how parts of your life have affected your way of thinking, and that you are not sure of what you want to do.

If you want to know *where is country*; in our country of Australia, it is well, *where country is.* It's with the land, *the springtime on the range* and the sea. It's the *spirit of Australia* and part of it, is with these diggers, both alive and dead. I believe it is the same in your country and all other countries in the world."

Come on, I'll take you back to town and you can work out if you want to go back to the States and your grandparents or if you want to stay here or keep travelling with me. The choice is yours to make."

As they walked away Johnny whispered "*So long, old mates* and thanks."

Back in town in the hotel dining room, Duncan sat at a table in the corner between the side wall and the big window from where he could see across the highway to the *lights on the hill* from the other vehicles that were either coming or going to their destinations.

Playing in the background, a *singer from down under* was singing *a song for the Aussies*. It was something about *rope and saddle blues*.

Near where he was sitting, a group of truck drivers were talking about some of the *long distance driving* that they do in the *outback*.

Then *Middleton's rouseabout* said "*The outback's not so wayback anymore. The overlander trail* from the *Three Rivers Hotel* to the *City Of Mt Isa* has just been sealed, now making it passable *when the rain*

23

tumbles down in July and *when bitumen reaches Pooncarie, Yellow Gully* road will be a short cut to *Woolloomooloo.*"

"I dunno." said *big John* "Getting through the lake country out there could be tough, especially *when the rain tumbles down in July.* You remember *bent-axle Bob*; well that's where he got his name from. He actually bent two axles driving on one stretch of road out there. He was taking a short cut from *Pooncarie* through to Mossgiel when it happened.

He was lucky that day 'cos an old Australian Bushman just happened to be driving through and gave him a lift to town. Not many *trucks* or other vehicles travel *way out there* and the two-way reception ain't much cop either. He would have had to *walk a country mile,* a long country mile if not for that bloke and *the Brass Well* nor any other kind of well exists out there either."

Kelly's offsider said "Did you hear about that guy in America whose sitting on *death row* for purposely letting a *king alligator* loose amongst some of his family and friends and how his kid wrote to the President saying "*I want a pardon for daddy.* Please *send back my daddy for Christmas.*"

This is not the first time he has tried to kill his family. They say that he drove an *old Kentucky rig* and had females all over the place, but after the kids he fathered got to a certain age, he would take off and leave them to fend for themselves or he would try to kill them."

"He'd be a *big beggin' fool* if he thought he could get away with it and I don't give him *a squatter's prayer* of getting off." said *Billinudgel.*

Kelly's offsider replied "A *bushman's prayer* would be too good for him. I would take him out and *leave him in the long yard* and see how he'd cope with a pack of wild *dogs* going for him and *when the Currawongs come down* to have their go, he'd soon be doing a *dolly dimple dance* around the place.

If I was the female, I'd be *walking on my way* right out of his clutches."

Then they all heard "*Looking forward looking back,* no, no, no. *Looking forward looking back,* no, no, no."

Middleton's rouseabout said "There goes *mad Jack's cockatoo* mouthing off again. Must be someone *dreamin' on the sliprail* nearby."

24

Kelly's offsider said "Just as long as they're not *road dreamin,* on the road. I haven't heard *mad Jack's cockatoo* mouthing off like that for some time now.

The last time he said something was when *old King Coal,* the guy who used to ride old Harlequin, took off with the *local Mary Magdalen* down the *long black road* towards the *Three Rivers Hotel* and *Charleville.*"

"Who's riding old Harlequin now?" asked one of the other driver's sitting at the table.

"A *ringer from the top end,* a bloke they call *wobbly boot* on account he is a *recycled ringer* who always has the *whiskey blues.*" came the reply.

Duncan stared in to his mug of coffee as thoughts of his own father, his mother, his old home and his grandparents came rushing into his mind. "I have *been a fool too long,* just *bumming around* and praying that *I'll be a bachelor till I die* is the wrong way to go about things.

Grandfather Johnson always said *"Getting away from it all* can help for a little while but then the *precious Lord* will find a way to get into a *runaway heart* and make that person stop and look inside themselves. It is *the nature of man* to run from some *trouble.*"

He also said *"When you're short of a quid, when you're short of a smoke* or *when your pants begin to go* and need replacing, something will happen that will get you through." he thought.

That night, for the first time since her death, Duncan dreamt of his mother, who was holding a *tiny blue shoe.*

She said to him "Darling, you have not *been a fool too long.* When I had you, you were the *baby of my dreams.* Yes, that's right, the *baby of my dreams* because I was told that I would never have children.

Andy's return, your father, from the war in the Pacific, put a strain on everybody around him. We could not mention anything about the war.

He never drank before he left, but he came back as if he had been *born with an endless thirst* and he always spent his *payday at the pub.* Even though we never talked about it, we all knew that his experiences during the war must have been horrific.

25

He wouldn't seek proper help, so we did the best we could at the time and for us, there was never *the answer to the pub with no beer* because he always found somewhere to drink.

Your great grandmother left me *an old fashioned locket* that I gave to my mother for safe keeping because your father wanted to sell it so he could buy alcohol with the money. *A fool such as I* should have known that marrying someone who was *born a travelling man* would not work out.

Yes, your father was never a *star trucker*, in fact he was a *no good truckin' man* but I did love him.

Please listen to those around you and don't let the *relics of the past* hurt you anymore. There are many good *memories* to look back on. *My son*, there are people who love you, send them a *letter from down under* from a *little boy lost* in hurt and anger and don't let this *lover's lament* stop you from loving someone.

To start *movin' on* in your life means *movin' away* from the past and letting the *joy bells in your heart* ring out loud enough to *keep the lovelight shining* for all to see. *Step down from this mountain* that you have climbed and become the man who you want to be.

When I first saw the love light in you eyes when you were born, I knew that you were *the pearl of them all*, of all the children born that day. It will be hard at first but with some perseverance, you will succeed.

I am in the *kingdom I call home* now, but I will still watch over you. I can't tell you what to do anymore, so you will have to choose for yourself, but the person who you could travel with, is *a friend indeed*, a real friend who won't let you go wrong."

Duncan woke and looked at the *faded coat of blue* that he had been wearing; lying across the kitchen chair and on it he saw a *little blossom*, just like the ones back home that were in *the valley where frangipanis grow* in the spring time.

He knew then what he wanted to do and where he wanted to go. He closed his eyes again and went back into a peaceful, dreamless sleep.

HOW DOES HE KNOW?

It was a cold morning as Duncan walked from his room to the dining area of the hotel. There he found Johnny sitting *by the fire of gidgee coal* drinking his coffee.

Johnny looked up as Duncan approached and said "After you have eaten, we'll get going. It's a long drive between here and Tamworth and I don't want to take too many breaks in between.

I also think it's about time you learnt to drive on these outback roads, so you can do the first stint behind the wheel of the *old sunlander van.* Don't worry about *waltzing Matilda* along the roads, she's easy to drive."

As Duncan sat down, he noticed another *little blossom*, the same kind that was on his coat when he woke after his dream, on the table.

Coming from somewhere outback, he heard "*Looking forward looking back*, no, no, no, look only at today. *Looking forward looking back*, no, no, no, look only at today."

"He's *taking his chance*, letting me drive." he thought, before he said "How did you know that I was going to continue travelling with you?" asked Duncan inquisitively to Johnny.

Johnny's reply was "*Did you think that I do not know* about life and people. I knew from the time I picked you up hitch hiking from under the *gumtrees by the roadway* that your life seemed to be travelling on the *last train to nowhere*, on a *lonesome road of tears*. I also know that you were not *born to be a rolling stone*, even though you've come from the *broken home side* of life.

When we reach Tamworth, we'll be there for a few days, so write your grandparents like your mother said, because to them, you are still *the pearl of them all.*"

Duncan looked stunned and said to Johnny "How do you know what my mother said? She only came to me in a dream last night; in fact, it was the first time since her death that I have dreamt about her."

Johnny smiled at Duncan and said "*Out of the blue gums I heard the bluebird sing.*"

"But...*Ah, forget it*. You're not going to give me a straight answer anyway. Are you?" griped Duncan.

Duncan handled the *long distance driving* without much difficulty, although it felt strange driving on the other side of the road, to which he was used to doing.

They passed a few *road trains* and a *roadliner* that had just turned right from out of *the Wave Hill track.*

"*When the sun goes down outback* and the *lights on the hill* ahead become brighter, you have to *slow down* your speed a bit." said Johnny. "*Some things never change out here.*

Once when I was mustering, in the old *horse and hobble days,* you could *saddle up and ride* the *stock horses* for days on end, and *Sat'day in the saddle* during *springtime on the range* was the best time of all. You never got the *rope & saddle blues* if you treated your horse and mates well. *The drover's cook* always fed us well, especially when he cooked *big yabbies from the creek* or *ribs cooked on the coals.*

I broke a promise to my parents and started driving a *big old Mack* truck. *Life behind the windscreen* was lonely and I started to miss the *old stock ridin' days* and *riding through the valley in spring.* I stopped driving rigs when I started to get the *road train blue*s and went back to a *drover's life.*

One day, whilst riding *down the dusty road to home,* I ran into *the man from Ironbark* and *the man from Snowy River* who was meeting *the man from the Never Never* and *Clancy of the Overflow* at *the Isa rodeo* and they invited me to ride with them."

As they drove through *another town,* Johnny said "Pull in *down at the Woolshed* Roadhouse and we'll have a break there.

We'll have some *good old country style home cookin'* before I take over the driving. *Jane O'Hara* is a *good hearted woman* and is the *Queen of hearts* to all who stop here. *The rose in her hair* is the same colour that you're mother sometimes wore when she was out dancing the *Missouri waltz.*"

As they sat down at a table near the middle of the roadhouse diner, Johnny turned up the radio and said "*This song is just for you.*"

Surprised by what Johnny had just said, Duncan asked "How do you know all this stuff about me and my folks?

This is *the hangover song*, the *music my dad played to me* and I have only seen photos of my mother with a rose in her hair.

My mother only told me twice, when I was young that *"our wedding waltz* was the Missouri waltz."

I'm gonna hump my bluey, as you would say, and find my own way to some bigger town if I don't get some straight answers from you."

Johnny replied *"Fair enough*, but wait a bit longer for me to answer your questions. You're not ready to know the answers yet."

They ate their meals and were soon back on the road to Tamworth, with Johnny driving and Duncan either looking at the countryside silently thinking *"I won't believe it's never gonna rain* on this dry land, even *when the rain tumbles down in July*, it must rain here at other times during the year." or nodding off for awhile.

They drove like they were *pushin' time* and Johnny knew many short cuts and by passes, so they only hit the outskirts of Collarenebri on their way to Gurley, where they stopped for mixed grills at the roadhouse before they continued on.

About an hour later, they left the roadhouse and this time it was Duncan's turn to drive.

Johnny said "Just past the *danger road train* sign, make a right turn onto the sealed road and follow it because it will take us to Bingara, where we'll spend the night."

Duncan turned right just past the sign, and then Johnny said "The *end of the bitumen* is about ten miles down the road and when you hit the dirt section, you may have to take it easy 'cos *when the rain tumbles down in July*, it washes out sections of the road.

That section of road is very much like the *end of the Canning Stock Route*, and you should reach the *Dinosuar* Road pass of the *Keela Valley* before dusk, and you will see the *lights on the hill* from the homesteads.

On the other side of the pass is *Mackenzie Country*. His story was very similar to you father, *Andy's return* from the war. Except one night, it was over a *Christmas at the station* of the *Commercial D.T's*, he had a *battle with a Roan* called *Goldy Girl* and was thrown from the horse; he was drunk at the time.

Many people used to say that he used to leave *a pub with no beer* left for anyone else because he was *born with an endless thirst*.

The following day, he was *down at Charlie Gray's* place and was *foolin' around* doing the *ringer's stomp*. It was just before he and the *cattlemen from the high plains* were about to set out *drovin'* some *cattle* to the *Eumerella Shores* station, when he collapsed. *The boss man* called the Flying Doctors who flew him to hospital. He had suffered head injuries from *the battle with the Roan*.

He was never the same when he went home from the hospital several months later and he passed away a few years later. I miss *my old pal Mack – a final tribute* to him was to rename his property Mackenzie Country."

Johnny fell silent and finally fell a sleep for awhile. Meanwhile, even when driving down the *middle of the road*, Duncan had to swerve at times to miss bad patches or pot holes. Duncan saw the *lights on the hill* at dusk, like he was told he would and before long, he was driving through the pass.

He passed a sign that read "*Keela Valley coals* and logs for sale. Next turn left".

Driving down the other side of the pass, Duncan thought "This is *where I want to be, when the sun goes down outback time and where the western clouds at sunset turn to gold. Even when the rain tumbles down in July,* this is *where country is.*"

It was another hour and a half before they drove into Bingara and Duncan noticed that on the outskirts of town, two *old time country halls* stood side by side and wondered why they were separate buildings that were so close together.

Duncan was startled when Johnny said "Stop at the *Boomerang* Hotel at the end of the main street. *Paddy William* makes the best stews and his pumpkin soup is so hot and thick, but his damper is made from an old family recipe, and it tastes so good.

While the damper cooks, we can clean up, I don't know about you, but *I'm dusty all over.*

We'll spend the night there so you can have a good rest from the driving you've done today.

It's about another two hours, 162 miles to Tamworth. I want to have a short stop in Manilla, about half way on the journey to Tamworth."

"How many kilometers is that?" asked Duncan.

"I dunno." said Johnny *"Kilometers are still miles to me.* You know when I drive into this town; it reminds me of *a town like Alice* Springs, small but friendly."

Just outside the hotel's door, Duncan heard the *Mareeba's rodeo song* playing across the road and *the Old Lantern Waltz* coming from inside the hotel and as they walked into the *Boomerang*, they heard the barman say "Do you want to give the *answer to Billy*; does anyone want to give the answer to Billy?"

"Give the answer to what?" asked Johnny.

The barman turned towards the door and said *"G'day G'day.* You know; the *answer to the old rusty bell* question."

As Johnny looked around the room, he commented *"Where's the old cobber of mine?"*

"He's down at one of the *old time country halls* with *Georgina's son*, setting up for *the Flying Doctor's ball* that's on tomorrow night." said one of the hotel patrons.

"Well, if *the Flying Doctor's ball* is on tomorrow, then that means that *the Foxleigh Rodeo* was on last weekend and *the annual rodeo show* and *country revival* will be on in Tamworth next week, starting with the *cattle camp reverie* at the show grounds. Well, let's say that Tamworth's style of reverie is really revelry, loads of music and dancing.

As for *my old pal, I'll meet him tomorrow* morning before we leave." said Johnny.

Duncan smiled to himself as other patrons burst out laughing when out of the blue, someone said *"The only time a fisherman tells the truth,* especially about the one that got away, is when he is holding the fish that got away."

In another part of the saloon bar, there were a group of men who were listening to the shearer's story and then started singing the shearing song.

"Hey Bob, what sort of terbaccy do you carry?" said a heavy set man.

"White Ox, Drum or Capstan." replied Bob.

"Give us a pouch of Drum. *That's my kind of brand. I must have good terbaccy when I smoke.*" said the heavy set man.

"*How will I go with him mate,* the dog's only been herding sheep for a short while?" asked a young man sitting at another table behind them.

"Just say *stick to him Bluey* very firmly. If he's been trained well, he'll obey the command and you shouldn't have any trouble." said an elderly man sitting opposite him.

RESTING PLACE

They left early that morning, so early, that Duncan had the *5am blues* and *a fire of gidgee coal* was still smoldering near the back of the car park. It was going to be just *another day* travelling down the highway, at least it was sealed this time, no more dirt roads, but best of all, Johnny was driving and the country side was a bit greener from *when the rain tumbles down in July* and other parts of the year.

As they left Bingara, Duncan saw the *lights on the hill* to the right, where the *spirit of Australia*, the people of the country was rising to start the day.

Somebody's mother would have been up for hours, baking bread or damper and preparing meals for their family and workers on their properties. She wouldn't have to worry about doing all that cooking *when they muster on the Golden Plain* because the *drover's cook* would attend to the meals. *Straight ahead*, Duncan could see the *lights on the hill* of the trucks descending, being turned off.

Johnny glanced at Duncan and said "We'll be in Tamworth in a few hours. When we get there, the first thing we'll do is find a place to stay for a week, and then we'll go down to Peel Street to see if Texas Jack is in his office. It's important for me to have *a word to Texas Jack* as soon as I can. I hope he got the letter I sent him via the *Abalinga Mail* run.

On the way through, we'll have a quick stop in Manilla 'cos I want to see *dribbler Bill* before the pub opens. *He's a good bloke when he's sober but* when he gets a few drinks in him, it's rather hard to get any sense out of him. *A pub with no beer* would be a good place for him to spend his days in."

Duncan's reply was "What am I going to do if I stay with you for a week in Tamworth. I know that you're doing some sort of business while we're travelling, but you still haven't given me an answer to how you know so much; especially about me?"

Johnny said "Now is not the time for answers, but I promise, when the time is right, I'll give them to you. You can leave once we reach Tamworth, however, I don't think you will because there will be so much going on, in and around town that you'll want to stay for the fun, excitement and the experiences that you'll have."

33

They spent a longer period of time in Manilla than they intended to, so while Johnny went looking for Bill, Duncan waited in a café drinking coffee.

He heard one teenage boy tell another boy "*When your pants begin to go*, don't get your mum to fix them, because the city fashion is pants that look well-worn and torn."

Looking around the café, Duncan noticed a painting of *Clancy of the Overflow* that was signed by *Namatjira*, a painting of a *saddle boy* standing under a *Sale day at St Lawrence* banner and a painting called *Springtime on the Range*. The last painting reminded him of *a picture of home* and mixed emotion came over him. He didn't get much time to dwell on the emotions because Johnny returned and was anxious to get back on the road again.

A little way down the road they passed a road sign that read "*ARCADIA VALLEY OLD TIME COUNTRY HALLS. TURN LEFT TOWARDS THE RED RIVER VALLEY*."

Once they reached Tamworth, Johnny headed for the *Cosy Inn*, in Bourke Street, run by *Annie Johnson*. The Inn was near a *pub with no beer* that was next to the railway line.

As they walked into the Cosy Inn's office, Annie looked at Johnny and said "*Hey good lookin'*, where have you been? Haven't seen you around here for a long time."

Then she looked past Johnny to Duncan and then back to Johnny and said "I have only two rooms left for a week if you want them? I would hate to see you left *high dry and homeless*. I know that you have your van but after *ridin' the road* for days on end, you need a comfortable resting place."

After they had settled in and cleaned up, Johnny and Duncan set out on foot for Texas Jack's office in Peel Street, which was one block away on the other side of the railway line from the Cosy Inn. It was good to be walking again instead of driving.

They easily found the office which was opposite the Town Hall, where *two singers* were singing a *song for the Aussies*, and Cheapa Music store.

Johnny said to Duncan "Once I've had *a word to Texas Jack*, we'll go over to the music store and say g'day to *my old pal* Col, Peter and the boys, and then I'll show you around the town.

34

Some of *my favourite people* will be gathering here in Tamworth this week for the music and rodeo.

Don't worry about having to drive; we'll be able to walk to most places around here and my intentions are for *losin' my blues* tonight and most nights."

They walked into the office and two men looked up from behind a desk and one, whom Duncan presumed to be Texas Jack said "*Hello trouble.* This is *Trumby* who has been working on the issue that you've asked me to look into for you for 'old home week'. We did receive the letter with the extra info you sent by the *Abalinga Mail* run.

Let's go into my office and we can talk there. You always come up with sticky situations, don't you?"

Trumby and Duncan stayed outside in the front office in silence before Johnny came out laughing with Texas Jack.

"We'll see you down at *Joe Maguire's pub* later on this arvo." Johnny said to Texas Jack, then said to Duncan "Let's go. C'mon, I'll show you around town."

Texas Jacks last words were "Next time, *why don't you go fishing* or rather stay fishing?"

They crossed the road and entered the music shop and Duncan couldn't believe his eyes, instead of records, tapes and CDs as he was expecting to see, this shop was full of musical instruments, sheet music and accessories for each instrument.

The different varieties of guitars alone astounded him. Some of the sheet music on display were *The Old Lantern Waltz, Sing Along With Dad, Yodel Down The Valley* and *There Lies A Workhorse.*

Johnny turned to Duncan and said grinningly, "Not what you expected to see, hey. *Country music's in our bones* and in the coming week, not only will there be a *country revival* going on around town and at the showground at night but during the day at the showground, a week long rodeo will be on. Even the racecourse holds special types of races during the day and on the Thursday night; *the Flying Doctor's ball* will be held country style."

Col approached Johnny saying "*G'day G'day*, good to see you back in town.

You're just in time because *tonight the woolshed swings* as there's a *travellin' country band* playing and there'll be a contest between *two singers* who have to sing *Waltzing Matilda* and do a *yodel melody*.

Johnny, *you and my old guitar* did a good rendition of *The Showman's Song* a few years back in the *good old days*. Do you wanna do it again this year?"

Duncan looked surprised at Johnny who said "Nah, I'm getting too old and the voice ain't the same anymore. I'm gonna be *losin' my blues* tonight if I can find somewhere to *sing a happy song* with someone who has a *travellin' guitar*. We'll catch up and have a coldie somewhere soon.

Right, you ready to go now Duncan. See ya Col."

When they left the shop, they went left and headed for the Toyota Country Marquis where some country singers were busking out front of it.

The rest of the afternoon was spent just wandering around town. From Kable Avenue, Duncan could see many caravans, tents, *tarps and trailers* being set up on both sides of the Peel River that ran through the town and some sunburnt people.

"One year, back in the *horse and hobble days*, a big wet happened *somewhere up in Queensland* and it affected much of the outback. *Something in the Pilliga* caused a landslide and *somewhere between* both places, the rivers flooded and the water suddenly came rushing through here washing out the campers. There were four *old time country halls* around Tamworth that were used to house the campers.

You can still see one of the *old time country halls* standing on the high ground over there and it still has the *old paint* on it as a reminder that *when the rain tumbles down in July* or if a big wet should hit up north, then the possibility of flooding could happen here.

Let's wander back to the Cosy Inn but we'll stop for a drink first at the Imperial *Callaghan's Hotel*. I hope that they still have their beer on tap.

For a week, both the Tamworth and Imperial Callaghan Hotels become *a pub with no beer*.

36

Oh, *the pubs still make a quid* because it's a popular place for the under aged teenagers to hang out in the evening. Both pubs use the family lounge room and adult supervisors because legally under aged kids are not allowed in a hotel or any where that sells alcohol unless they are under adult supervision. They also get a special written approval to do it.

Ever *since the Bushland Boogie came this way*, the *Ringer's Stomp* is no longer popular and *as the bush comes to town*, the teenagers needed a place to go to do their own kind of singing and dancing, you know *teenage country style*.

Believe it or not, but a few years back, I volunteered with an *old beau* to be a supervisor at the Imperial Callaghan for a night and being an *old rock 'n' roller* myself, I had fun watching the kids do *rock 'n' roll in a cowboy hat*.

Two little girls in blue made *the pub rock* when they first sang *the ballad of Port Macquarie* in an upbeat tempo then did *the ballad of Henry Holloway* as a *modern yodelling song*.

One of the girls sung as if she was one of *God's own singer of songs* and the other could *yodel down the valley* and make it sound like *Heaven country style*. She must have been *born to be a yodeller* and at the time I felt like *losin' my blues tonight* and I did."

The first thing that everyone saw as they walked into the Imperial Callaghan Hotel was the *smiles* on the faces in the painting of *Granny's Hieland Hame's* family hanging on the wall that was decorated with *Stringybark and greenhide*. Next to the painting, was a poster pointing out the *ten golden rules* for the teenagers to abide by.

Looking towards the back wall, Duncan noticed another *ten golden rules* poster tacked to the wall beside a painting of *Suvla Bay* at *sundown* and a few words that read "*dear old sunny south by the sea*". Along the back wall, a stage was built for the bands that were going to be playing over the next week; however, at that moment, there was music being played on a *Regal Zonophone*, a *wind up gramophone* that sounded kinda funny when it needed re-winding.

The peace in the hotel was broken as the men from the *Cobb and Co. Twitch* station walked in talking to each other.

"Did you *leave him in the long yard?*" said one of them.

"Yeah." said another "But I should have tied him to the *leaning post* instead and maybe *Lawson's ghost* would come and pay him a visit."

Then one of the men spotted Johnny and said "*G'day blue*, fancy meeting you here. Come for the rodeo or the music? I see you still have Duncan with you; he couldn't be as bad as what we've had to travel with."

"*Tex Morton*, what are you blokes doing way down here? Both, the music and rodeo but tonight *I'm losing my blues.* I also want to catch up with some old mates if they're still around.

Have you still got *that old blue dog of mine?*" said Johnny.

"Sorry Johnny, he was *just an old cattledog* and he passed a year ago.

We've come for the rodeo and *the clearing sale*. We've got six *trucks on the track*. Unfortunately a *Middleton's rouseabout, Marty* came down with us and he would be *the greatest Australian whinger*, that's for sure. We should teach that *Marty* a lesson and make him a *rodeo clown* for the day when the *rough riders* go out in the *rough ridin' rodeo* part.

If I were free tonight, *I'll be steppin' too.*" said Tex.

"Any others come down with you?" asked Johnny.

"In one truck was a *Cunnamulla fella* and the others had *Harry the breaker*, a *ringer from the top end*, a *territory ringer* and the *son of noisy Dan* who is nothing like his father.

We nick named him *St Peter* 'cos he brought his *travellin' guitar* with him and played some *old time music* for us. He's really good and when he played the *Orange Blossom Special*, it took me back to the time of *Charley Gray's Barndance* where I met the *mountain man's girl, Murrumbidgee Rose*. I wish that I had never had to say *hello and goodbye* to her in a matter of a few hours."

Sitting beside them, another one of the men said "Not that one, the other one. *I must have good terbaccy when I smoke.*"

Tex looked at Duncan and said "If you are not doing anything important tomorrow, do you wanna meet me down at the show ground and you can give us a hand for awhile and I'll teach you a bit about

38

stock horses and *rodeo riders. St Peter* can tell you a thing or two about *the old saddle* and he should know what he's talking about because *the saddle is his home* for most of the year."

Duncan looked surprisingly at Johnny, who then said *"Give it a go, mate.* Tex here is one of the best in the business and he has *Harry the breaker* with him.

When the rain tumbles down in July, handling different animals and machinery is not as easy as it looks, especially *when the scrubbers break.*

You can learn a lot from both of them and it'll be a handy thing to know if you want to stay and work here in Australia."

They sat there talking and drinking for a while longer, then an exhausted pair (Johnny and Duncan) headed back to the Cosy Inn for a good nights sleep.

It was a beautiful, crisp morning when Duncan joined Johnny for breakfast.

Both men had had a good nights sleep and had woken relaxed and in high spirits.

Over breakfast, the conversation of what they intended to do that day arose and the worried expression on Duncan's face also carried through to his voice when he asked *"How will I go with him, mate?*

Back in *Camooweal*, I heard so many stories about the things that are done on the different stations and especially how good and knowledgeable *Harry the breaker* is. His reputation around there was as big as *Holydan*, one of our countries leading *roughriders* was."

"Don't you worry about that." said Johnny "I have known both Tex and Harry for many years and if Tex didn't think that you could handle the work, he wouldn't have said anything.

I remember when *Clancy of the Overflow, the man from Iron Bark, the man from Snowy River, the man from the Never Never* station, a *Cunnamulla feller* and myself met at an *old woolshed ball* in *old Tiboob'ra.*

Together we travelled to *the Foxleigh Rodeo* and the *Isa Rodeo*, then travelled down to Port Augusta on the *Sunlander* train and across on the

Indian Pacific train to Perth for *the Rutland Rodeo. The Sunlander* doesn't go down that far anymore.

When the *Rutland Rodeo* was over, we all went our own ways. *Clancy of the Overflow* and I travelled back on the *Indian Pacific* and on *the Sunlander* where we met Harry.

Harry Bowden...derelict is now *Harry the breaker* and he has earned every bit of his reputation through his hard work, his working ethics and the respect he gives to everyone else.

He's just the one you need to teach you. *Many mothers* would give the *Murray moon* to have the likes of Tex and Harry teaching their sons because they are *the vanishing breed* of station managers.

Enough of that, it's starting to sound like *the swagman's story* and anyway *that was years ago*. Now I have a gift for you."

Johnny handed Duncan a hat and added "Now, *about this hat*, it was given to me by a *sunny northern Rose* who was in her *sunset years of life*. I stopped at her property, *Gymkhana Yodel*, just as she was coming out of the house to collect some *old river gum* logs for her fire.

As she looked at me I asked *"Can I sleep in your barn tonight?"* I didn't have Matilda at that time.

Still looking at me, she asked "Did you *walk a country mile* today?" and when I told her that I had, she said *"Good Heavens above*, you look like you could do with a good feed and a long bath. Now you just *walk right in* there and sit down at *the round table* and I'll fix you something to eat."

She sent for her station manager, *Henry Lawson* who gave me a room in *the old sundowner* house and some work. Henry told me that *when a boy from Alabama meets a girl from Gundagai* and they get married and build a property together, you would think that they would be happy.

To the Alabama guy it seemed that *love's a game of let's pretend* as one day she found a strange *black velvet band* in his jeans pocket and confronted him about it.

She said to him *"You stepped out of line."* and he replied that the owner of the band was just an *anyday woman* but refused to name her and said that he was leaving.

Her reply to him was "*Give my love to Sydney town* 'cos I know that's where you're off too."

When the country's wet, grain grows and the cattle have lush green grasses to graze on, but in *drought time*, nothing grows. I think that *the biggest disappointment* for her was when she had to send some of her workers to work for *Cobb and Co. Twitch*.

I refused to go and it's a good thing I did, because a month later, the *dry weather wind* blew a *Willy Willy* this way.

That was no ordinary *Willy Willy* but one that was as strong as those tornados that they have in the States."

"*When the harvest days are over*" said Johnny "You have to find work else where, so I left. Years later I found out that in *the bequest* from Rose, I was given *Henry Lawson's pen*. I never did find out what happened to *Gymkhana Yodel* Station.

I didn't wear that hat much either, because my *sunny southern Sue* gave me this one, and that's another story for *another day*."

"I tried settling down but *that's not me. When the rain tumbles down in July, when the Currawongs come down, when it's lamplighting time in the valley or when Snowy sings of home*, it doesn't make any difference to me because *the road is still my home* and *you can't tell me a thing* that would make me change my mind."

COUNTRY LIFESTYLES

During the next two days, Duncan saw many *ringers rigs & drivers*, and Harry teach some young farm hands how to brand cattle the right way, with the *D towards the head*. Harry then turned to Duncan and said "Now you *give it a go*."

"Me!" exclaimed Duncan "*How will I go with him mate?* I have never handled cattle before."

"Just do as I told the other young lads to do. That's right, not too hard; put the *D towards the head*."

Everyday he smelt *dust and diesel, dust and saddle grease* and food cooking on an *old bush barbeque* somewhere nearby. He often heard people practicing tunes like *Our Wedding Waltz, the Bushland Boogie* and *Tie Me Kangaroo Down Sport*.

"*That's the song we're singing* with the *Travellin' Country Band.*" said a middle aged woman to her young children's choir who was just walking past.

One evening, he couldn't help overhearing a young couple arguing as he walk passed them in the shadows. They were standing *by the fire of gidgee coals* when the man said to the female "Maybe *I've been a fool too long.* I saw you with *Dan the wreck* at the *Binieye Ball*, and you weren't doing the *Claypan Boogie* either."

"At least I wasn't *drowning my blues* at the bar again. Lately all I see of you is the *man in the glass*, drinking in some *memory hotel. Oh, Sydney I love you* by *my love's a stranger now*.

So *I'm layin' it on the line*, you had better shake those *brown bottle blues* or I'm going back to *Charleville* without you."

Duncan thought "Oh, another *prairie loveknot* to be undone."

He then heard "*Jessie dear, give me one more chance*, you know *I love my truck* but *I love you best of all*. Sometimes when I get the *highway blues*, I remember *the day I married you* and that *I got you* waiting for me back in *my old Aussie homestead* and I feel *as good as new* again. *Pushin' time* in *my blue Pacific rig along the road to Nulla Nulla*, makes me feel that my *dieseline dreams* will soon come true because I'm nearly home, *back where I belong*, with you."

A softly spoken reply was heard coming from the female "*Don't fool around anymore* with those silly thoughts, *you took the joy out of living* and *I'm lonesome for Sydney tonight*, my Sydney, the one who used to tell me that I put the *joy bells in your heart. I need somebody to hold me when I cry* not someone who makes me cry."

Holding her close, he said "*Jessie dear, I'm still here to give it my best. I'm like a boomerang* 'cos I keep coming back to you. Now are we *going to the barn dance tonight?* Come on, put that sweet smile back on your face, you *sweet thang.*"

She replied "*How can I smile when I'm lonely?*"

"Look, I'll go tell *Middleton's rouseabout* not to *leave him in the long yard* but to stable *Silver Spurs* tonight. *You'd better be waiting* for me in that pretty blue dress and your *lace-up shoes* so we can go and dance to *our wedding waltz*, the *Arajoel waltz* and *the bushland boogie.*"

A short distance from the edge of the camp, Duncan heard the roar of laughter coming from *The Decimal Currency Pub* and decided to investigate what was causing so much laughter.

Upon entering the pub, he heard one of the *bush poets of Australia* reciting his own version of *a sequel to a pub with no beer* and looking around at the patrons, he decided that this was definitely not *a pub with no beer.*

He went to the bar and purchased a middy of beer and as it was placed in front of him, someone shouted "*You've got to drink the froth to get to the beer.*"

Roars of laughter started up again.

Duncan thought to himself again "Yep, this is definitely not *a pub with no beer.*"

"*G'day G'day*. Are you on your way back to the Cosy Inn?"

Duncan turned to see *Trumby* behind him, and then Trumby added "He's not only one of the best *bush poets of Australia* but he's also one of the *best balladeers of Australia* because his renditions of the *Ballad of the Drover* and *the Ballad of big Bill Smith* are so comical.

43

I also like his version of *the Answer to the Pub with no beer*, 'cos in the end he says that the reason for *a pub with no beer* is that the *ghosts of the Golden Mile* rode the *Glory Bound train* to it and drank it all.

When you see Johnny, could you tell him to come to the office please? We have some of the information that he was after."

Duncan arrived back at the Cosy Inn at the same time as Johnny.

Duncan passed on the message from Trumby to Johnny who then said "How's it going for you? Haven't seen you for the last couple of days?"

Duncan went into the dining room and had coffee with Johnny, telling him all that he saw, how Harry had taught him the right way to brand cattle, the near *lover's lament* that he had overheard and the meeting with Trumby at the pub.

Then Duncan said "Harry's taking me to the sale yard and to the rodeo and races. I've never been to any of them so it should be interesting."

Johnny replied "Watch out for *old Scobie, the retired drover* from the *Plains of Peppimenarti*. He's good with *the drover's yarn* and most of what he says is true.

If he's not at the sale yard, then he'll be in *the front row* with all the *old riders in the grandstand*. He will be *the man with the hat turned down in front* and if you do see him, go and introduce yourself to him and tell him that Johnny says hello *to an old mate* and *three times seven* at the *Three Rivers Hotel*. It may sound weird but tell him as he will understand the meaning.

Tomorrow night, if you're not too exhausted, would you like to come with me to the Imperial Callaghan Hotel as a volunteer because it will be their first night as *a pub with no beer* and will *the pub rock*.

A new local country band called *Top Springs* will be playing their new song *the Snake Gully Swagger*. Have you ever seen or done the *Beer Barrel Polka* rock and roll style?"

The next day at the sale yards, Harry did the i*ntroduction* all round.

Kelly's offsider asked Harry why there were *no bids for the bay* and Harry told him that it was lame and wouldn't even be able to carry a *saddle boy* very far without breaking down.

They left the sale yard and walked over to where the races were being held.

The first race was for *the old bullock dray* teams. One team wouldn't pull up at the start line, even after the driver yelled out "*Whoa, bullocks whoa*" and delayed the start by a couple of minutes but after the races got under way, the shouts of "*Whoa, bullocks whoa*" were heard again, as another team of bullocks headed for some open *gates*.

In the fourth race, there was a lady rider and Harry said "The girl's name is *Isa*, short for Isabella and she's riding *Foggy Mirrors*, the best horse here. I wonder if she's as good *back in the saddle* as she used to be.

Isa, well, *the lady is a trucker, the last of her line*, but she learnt all the skills that most men learn on the station, *Anthill Style*, the property once owned by *old Dan, the man from the Never Never* station.

Sure enough, Isa won the race and as the cheers went up; Duncan looked around and spotted old Scobie in *the front row* of the grandstand.

Duncan did as Johnny requested and introduced himself to Scobie and said "Johnny told me to say hello *to an old mate* and *three times seven* at the *Three Rivers Hotel* and that you would understand the meaning."

With the biggest smile that Duncan had ever seen and with tears in his eyes, Scobie said "Hello Duncan, it's a pleasure meeting you and thanks for bringing me the message. I'm not as young as I used to be and I'm riding a *bucking horse called Time*.

One *Christmas, when I was big as you*, I met Johnny at a *country revival*, right here in Tamworth. At the time we were both *game as Ned Kelly*, Ah! the *good old days*.

You know *I've been, seen and done that*, both Johnny and I have met *King Bundawaal* and the *King of Kalgoorlie* on the *Indian Pacific*, the only time we went *droving by train* and together we've seen *every little bit of Australia*.

At the *Nebo pub*, I was offered work with *the man from Snowy River* as *the man who steadies the lead* horse in a mob of wild brumbies and Johnny just wanted to keep travelling. We kept in touch for awhile when Johnny tried to settle down, but he was never good at staying in one place for long.

At one time, I heard that he went to *Goldrush country* in Victoria, but even that didn't last long."

Duncan's surprised look made Scobie say "He hasn't told you anything, has he?"

Duncan replied "No, not much about himself but he promised he will when the time is right."

"Oh…that explains the message then. Has he been in contact with Texas Jack since you've been here?" asked Scobie.

"Yes." said Duncan, "as soon as we got here."

"May I ask, who else have you met through Johnny?" asked Scobie.

Duncan thought a bit then said "Jimmy Woodser, an indigenous elder, Indigo Jones, his translator, two old gentlemen who were the last two surviving rats of Tobruk in that area, Dick and Ivanhoe, Tex Morton and Harry the breaker and now you.

He has met other people along the way, but I wasn't with him then, he left me drinking coffee in a diner or café."

Scobie looked at Duncan and asked "Why are you travelling with Johnny and where are you going?"

"Well." said Duncan "I don't really know, it just feels right and there are questions that I want answers to. Where am I going; I guess it looks like *I'm going to Yarrawonga,* wherever that is?"

Scobie looked past Duncan and said quickly and softly, "Let me tell you, Johnny has been *a cattle camp crooner, a fiddle man,* he's been *drovin'* with the *cattlemen from the high plains,* a *ringer from the top end* of Australia, *the drover's cook* and he'll be *the last of the bushmen. We've been trucking too* and he'll be *the world's last truck drivin' man.*

Just remember son, *a mate can do no wrong,* if he's a true mate like Johnny. Considering all that we have done over the years, *we've done us proud.*"

"G'day, did I hear someone say my name. Are you boring young Duncan here with your *oldtime drover's lament?"* asked Johnny.

46

"*How's your memory?*" asked Scobie.

"Not too bad." said Johnny "*How's your memory?*"

"Remember *the dog who stole my hat?* Well, he was a *good hard dog* and a pal to me for many years and when he passed, I buried him in the spot *where the dog sits on the tucker box.* Where are you off to now?" asked Scobie.

"*I'm going back again to Yarrawonga, just going home.*" said Johnny.

"You staying put this time?" inquired Scobie.

"Nah, *give me the road* anytime, *travellin' still, always will.* Where are you living now?" asked Johnny.

"*The biggest disappointment* of my life was when I had to sell *that old bush shanty of mine* and move into that *shanty on the rise*, the *old men's home*, to live out my *sunset years of life.* It's been renovated from one of those *old time country halls* to a place where the *Aussie doghouse blues* live in everyone there.

If only I had a home sweet home to go to, then my *life's ride* would be complete. *In my hour of darkness*, I will have no regrets, *cause I have you* to thank for your special kind of friendship. I know that the *far grandest homestead of all* waits for me and we both know it, 'cos it's in the *Bible of the Bush.*" said Scobie.

"Don't talk like that; you're beginning to sound like *Brigalow Bill* with his *cattle camp reverie* yabber. You'll be doing the *Humpty Doo waltz* for a few years to come. *I haven't changed a bit* but *I guess you have* because you're always around older men who have not lived the life you have. C'mon, let's do something together. Now, where do want to go?" snapped Johnny.

"*Lead me down to the stock yards.* I want to see what horses they have for the rodeo tomorrow and find out whose riding what horse?" said Scobie.

It didn't take them long to walk down at the stockyard, and a list of horses was up on the board. Johnny explained to Duncan that these were buckin' broncos and were hard to ride.

47

A group of guys were talking around the board. *"Who wants Moss? Anyone, who wants Moss?"* no-one answered.

"Just saddle old Darky for me?" came a voice from the back.

"Nardoo Burns seems high spirited, so I'll ride him." came a voice from the front.

"I think that the *wild colonial boy* from *Camooweal* should ride *Whiplash."* came a voice from the middle of the group. "He thinks he's grouse, so let's see if he's just a show pony or not."

They left Scobie listening to the *Hooks & Ride Travelling Country Band* playing some *old time country songs*.

As they walked away, Johnny said "He's the *last of the Bushmen* surviving since the First World War. When he retired, he *took his saddle home* and placed it on an *old rocking horse*. He will never believe that he is *a prouder man than you* because every person does things that they can be proud of.

For most people, the *last thing to learn* in life is how to get ready to pass on but Scobie has learnt and is ready for when the time comes."

That evening at the Imperial Callaghan Hotel, Duncan was impressed with the way that both the teenagers and the hotel staff interacted with respect for each other. Duncan turned to Johnny and shouted "This band is good. They really know how to *rock this joint."*

UNEXPECTED NEWS

Over breakfast, Duncan and Johnny discussed what each would be doing that day. As Duncan was getting up from the table to leave, Johnny said "I'm going into town for a bit so I'll meet you at the rodeo."

Duncan was half way through the campsite, when he heard a child call to his parent "Mum, *I'm gonna take my dog for a run.*"

On the other side of the campsite, he heard *Kelly's offsider* yell "*Leave him in the long yard* for now."

"Hey mister, have you seen *the paper boy* anywhere in the campsite?"

Duncan turned to see a boy about nine years old holding onto the reins of a pony and a young girl aged about six years old standing beside him.

"No I haven't seen *the paper boy* today. Why do you ask?" asked Duncan.

"Dad asked me and Angela to find him and ask him to call at our tent." said the boy.

Duncan walked over and patted the pony on his nose and asked what the pony's name was.

The little boy replied "This is *my pony Whipstick*, that's my sister Angela, but mum calls her *the angel of Goulburn Hill*, dunno why and I'm *Jack O'Hagan.*"

"*Jack O'Hagan*, Angela. How many times have I told you not to wander around with your pony? If someone spooks it, how are you going to control him?" came a voice from a *sweet talking* woman who was walking up from behind all of them.

"Mum, I can handle him; don't forget I'm a *saddle boy* now." said Jack.

"That doesn't mean you're stronger than the pony. Oh, I'm sorry. I'm Beth O'Hagan and these are my children." said Beth.

Duncan looked at Beth with a curious but surprised look on his face and said "I'm Duncan."

Beth said "That accent, are you from the United States? You know, I was born there, but I grew up here in Australia with my two older brothers, Peter and Roy. Sorry, gotta get moving and get things ready for the rodeo."

As she walked away, Beth thought to herself, "*I've seen his face before but I can't remember where.*"

Duncan stood there watching as she walked away and thought to himself "If I didn't know better, I could swear that that woman was a younger version of my mother. Her hair, her looks, her eyes and her smile are just like moms were when I saw photos of her with my grandparents."

At the rodeo site, Duncan found Harry with a group of *rodeo riders* discussing their mounts and the tactics that they would each use for their events.

"*How will I go with him, mate? Indian Pacific* is a new brumby and it will be his first event." said one of the stocky riders.

Harry replied "*Indian Pacific* may be new, but you have ridden new brumbies before, so this one is no different. Just remember what you've learnt over the years and who, is *the boss*, out there in the ring. If you think that *Indian Pacific* will be a tough ride, then the *rough riders* have tougher rides on *the Bogong* and *the Crow*. *The Crow* was hard to round up because he kept sweeping in and out of the trees so an adaption to *the desert lair* had to be used in capturing him."

Harry saw Duncan and called him over to the group. An *introduction* was made by Harry and then he asked the riders if they had any objections to Duncan spending time with them.

No objections were given.

Harry said to Duncan "*The biggest disappointment* that I have these days, is that I can't ride with them anymore. *The battle with the Roan* at *the Isa Rodeo* was *the last ride* I ever had. Riding in a rodeo was *the happiest day of all* the year through, even happier than the time I broke *the bull stag* at *Tibrogargan* in Queensland."

The morning was pleasant and exciting. The *Cunnamulla feller* won his event on a brumby called *Breakaway* and *Indian Pacific* won his event. After the bronco riding had finished, the *introduction* for the cattle roping was made, with *Kelly's offsider* being the first up.

"*How will I go with him mate?* I've never ridden *Natural High* in the cattle roping arena before." said Kelly's offsider.

"You'll have no worries with him. He's easily ridden if you give him a little rein." said Kelly.

Duncan spotted Jack with his pony by a guardrail and went over to him and Jack said "*My pony Whipstick* and I are in the junior events that start when these have finished. Will you still be here to watch?"

At the end of all the adult events, the *ringer from the top end* was the overall champion receiving a trophy that looked like a mini version of *The Brass Well*.

Whilst Duncan was watching the junior events, Johnny sneaked up on Duncan and startled him by saying "C'mon, let's go and get a drink."

Duncan was about to object to going so soon, but something in the tone of Johnny's voice stopped him. They walked in silence until they reached *Joe Maguire's pub* and when they were *sitting on the old front veranda*, in a secluded spot, Johnny slipped Duncan an envelope and said "Read this and then I will answer a couple of questions for you."

Duncan opened the envelope and started reading the letter inside.

"Darling Duncan, We're so glad that you're alright, grandfather and I have been so worried about you. A gentleman from Arrabury Lawyers paid us a visit and told us of your whereabouts and said that if we wanted to write you, he would make sure you would get the letter. I don't know how he will find you?

I wish that we could have had this talk face to face, but distance and time won't allow it.

I suppose that you have heard about the man sitting on death row for trying to kill his family. Well, I'm sorry to have to tell you this, but it's your father. I have *been a fool too long* thinking that you'd never find out.

There is something else that you should know; you have an older sister somewhere, maybe over there in Australia. My youngest sister married an Australian feller named Dan and they had two sons, *Roy* and Peter while they were living here in the States.

Just after your mother was married, she fell pregnant and knowing that your father didn't want any children, came back here on a visit.

51

While she was here, your father was called up to join the marines and while he was away at the training camp, your mother gave birth to a beautiful little girl. Knowing what your father would say and do if he found out about your sister, your mother gave her daughter to my youngest sister to bring up.

Her husband Dan said "*I've got a possie way back in Aussie* and *lady luck* stepped in just in time because your sister's adoption went through a week before your father returned. They named your sister Beth and moved to Australia.

When she was old enough, Beth was told about her adoption and when your mother passed, I sent her a photo of your mom and the locket that she had given me for safe keeping. In the locket, your mother had placed two small photos, one of you and one of your sister.

Your father never knew about your sister but when you came along, your father didn't seem to mind because he was always out on the road travelling from place to place and when he was home, all he would say was "*My pal alcohol* and I won't be around for long."

Your sister looked so much like your mother and would be a couple of years older than you. The last time I saw her was when she left as a baby *on the night train* to New York on the eve of them leaving for Australia, going to live somewhere *west of Winton*.

Duncan, your grandfather and I are now in the *sunset years of life* and we felt that you should know the truth and reveal our secret. I hope you don't think of us as terrible people because *in my hour of darkness*, I would have hated taking that secret with me. Please forgive us and keep in contact occasionally. We both love you very much. Grandma".

Duncan slipped the letter back into the envelope and he noticed that it was addressed to "*To Whom It May concern*".

Duncan said "How did you know about my sister and how to contact my grandparents?"

Johnny replied "I have known Dan O'Hagan for many years and we have spent a lot of time together. When you told me your story, I wondered if your mother was the same person that Dan mentioned when he spoke about Beth one time.

I started the ball rolling back at Jambalaya, but I wasn't really sure until I met with Texas Jack in his office.

52

I didn't want to say anything until I had solid proof in my hands, especially *after all* that you've been through.

When we met with Jimmy Woodser by chance, and he told you that dream time story, then I knew that I was on the right track. Jimmy just knows about things, I don't know how he knows, but he just does.

Your sister is married to the other *son of noisy Dan*. There were two Dans in the same family, one was a quiet person, and the other, well you can guess by his nickname, he wasn't quiet.

Now, I know your sister, not very well mind you, but I can arrange a meeting with her if you want it and if I can find her."

Duncan just sat staring at the envelope for awhile, then quietly said "I think I have met her, this morning at the campsite."

Then he proceeded in telling Johnny about what had happened. Duncan added "When I first saw her, I was taken aback by how much she looked like my mother and when she introduced herself, it felt like she had *the softest touch in town*. She was so beautiful and to answer your question, yes, I would like to meet and spend time with her, if she wants to meet me."

Johnny said "If she is staying at the campsite, I'll find her and have a talk with her. She doesn't know about you, and if she wants to meet you, then I'll arrange for all of us to meet somewhere for drinks tonight. Now, where will you be for the next couple of hours?"

"I'll stay here for a bit, then I'll go back and find Harry and stay with him. I need something stronger to drink, maybe a whiskey." said Duncan.

"Now, don't go getting yourself the *whiskey blues* 'cos that won't help at all." warned Johnny. "I'll see you later. OK."

Back at Joe Maguire's pub later that evening, Duncan met his sister Beth properly for the first time and she was wearing his mother's locket; the one that his mother had left with his grandmother.

"I'm feeling a bit awkward at the moment and *I bet you feel the same.*" he thought to himself as he looked over to Beth.

FAMILY REUNION

A nervous Duncan walked onto the front veranda where an equally nervous Beth and her family were sitting. Johnny made the *introduction* and everyone seemed to relax a little. Duncan was really glad that this was not *a pub with no beer* because a beer was what he really needed at that moment.

Beth brought along the picture of her mother sitting at *the spinning wheel* that belonged to her grandmother.

As Duncan looked at the photo, he thought "*If those lips could only speak* what would they say?"

After a couple more drinks all round, everyone seemed to relax and the conversation flowed freely. *Nobody heard* the disagreement, in the background, over whether *Ned Kelly was a gentleman* or not.

Angela asked Duncan "Does *good old Santa Claus* still come to you? You know *Santa's gonna come in a mail coach* this year because where we live is too hot for his reindeers to fly."

Then Jack said "Angela can't see that *Santa looked like daddy* did last year."

Beth then said to Duncan "I always felt that I had a sibling somewhere, but all the attempts that I made, failed to bring any results, so I ended up, giving up my *Spanish pipe dream*. Now that we've met, please don't *stay away from me* or my family, you can be a *swagless swaggie* when you visit. That is if you ever want to?"

Duncan thought "How *good it is* to find some family. *A fool such as I* would be, to let this chance pass me by. *Are the good days gone forever?* I don't think that they've even started yet. *My life's getting better all the time.*"

Then he asked "Is your property anywhere near *Charleville?*"

"Oh no." said Beth. "It's further north and much more *further out.* Coming here each year for the *country revival* is a holiday for us. I would love to sit here and talk with you all night, but I think that we had better *get along*, back to the campsite and put these two tired children to bed.

Tomorrows a fun day at the showground, so do you want to spend the day with us?"

54

As she was getting up from the table, Duncan nodded his head yes and then she spotted Col, from the music shop, walking towards her carrying a guitar.

Col said "Johnny, Duncan." and acknowledged them with a nod of his head. "Beth I thought that you might want this guitar for tomorrow. I had a feeling you'd be here tonight. Oh, and *happy anniversary*, how long have you been married now?"

Beth smiled and said "Thank you for remembering, it's been ten years tomorrow and thank you for bringing *my son's guitar* to me tonight. I'll come in tomorrow and pay you for the repairs."

She looked at Duncan and said "*My son's guitar* was damaged last month at the *old woolshed do* when a *cattle camp crooner* accidentally dropped it while he was *pickin' and singin'* the *Song of Macleay* or the *Song Of The Macleay*, I never can remember the right name and the *song of the west* called *Westward ho!*. and there wasn't anywhere up where we live to get it fixed so I bought it here 'cos I knew Col could do the repairs quickly.

C'mon you two, it's time to *get along* to bed. We're going to have a big day tomorrow and Duncan and Johnny are going to be joining us, so say good night."

As Beth and her family walked away with Col, Duncan turned to Johnny and said "A couple of times I have asked myself "*What am I doing in this town?*" but I couldn't answer that question.

I thought last night that after this week it's time to be *wingin' my way back home*, but there's nothing really back there for me now. I will never see *the silver in my mother's hair* and in a few years, my grandparents will be gone.

The *country livin'* here is so great and the way the people are so friendly towards each other, and this *country revival* and the rodeo show each year is for everyone even if you are from a big city.

If I only had a home sweet home to settle down in, one where I can see hills that would remind me of the *hills of home* and the *pastures of home* beneath them. I'd even be more than happy to renovate one of those *old time country halls* into a homestead.

I'm thankful to you for finding my sister, who I never knew existed. Now *the biggest disappointment* I'm going to have is when I have to leave and go back home. Settling down here is *still the way I feel* and where I want to be."

"*I'm going back again to Yarrawonga.*" said Johnny "Why don't you still come with me. You can have an *old time Christmas* with us and with the *return of the stockman* and when *the drovers are back* from The Birdsville Track, we'll have a great time. I swear that when the *old woolshed do* gets underway, they can hear us all the way over at *Botany Bay*.

Why worry now about what might happen further down the track. Just enjoy tomorrow with Beth and her family and then we'll be on our way the day after."

Morning comes early for the country people and so does the *morning mail*. Duncan received a letter from the Immigration Department wanting any extra information that might help him regarding his residency application.

When he showed Johnny the letter, Johnny said "It's too early to see Texas Jack in his office, so take the letter with you because we're bound to run into him sometime today at the showground.

I'm looking forward to catching up with many *old bush mates of mine* and I'm guessing that you want to be with Beth and her family again, you must be on a *natural high* knowing that you're not alone anymore."

One of the first things that Duncan said to Beth when meeting her at her tent site was "*Happy Anniversary,* ten years today. With the way my life is now, I think that *I'll be a bachelor till I die.*"

"Don't be so certain." said Beth "See that young woman over there with the brown fringed jacket on her arm, that's *Barb'ry Allen*. If *you take her from Narrandera* to live near *Mount Bukaroo* or to live on the *Plains Of Peppimenarti, when the Currawongs come down* and *when it's lamp lighting time in the valley*, she would be the one to show you *where country is* and would tame *the wild life you lead*. Most country girls are like that especially if you treat them right."

They were interrupted by Jack saying "Come on mum, I want to see if Duncan can put *an axe mark on a gidgee* stump or see if he's as *game as Ned Kelly* and try to ride *Indian Pacific.*"

Duncan replied "Me! Ride *Indian Pacific*. If I did, you would have to *bury me beneath the willow* tree over there."

There was so much happening at the showground when they got there. Duncan saw Scobie in *the front row* of the grandstand laughing at a *cattle camp crooner's* version of *a sequel to the pub with no beer.*

Since the Bushland Boogie came this way and the younger generation wanted to learn different dances, The *Black Cotton Strand* dancers were teaching a group of teenagers *the Snake Gully Swagger* for *the rodeo dance* for teenagers in *the Man From Iron Bark* pavilion that night.

The Man From Snowy River pavilion was holding *the rodeo dance* for the families with younger children, and where *Mangrove Boogie Kings* would be playing.

In front of *the Man From The Never Never* pavilion, there were people setting up for the good *old bush barbeque* for every one to enjoy, with the proceeds of the sales going to the Flying Doctors.

He also saw posters that read *"TONIGHT THE WOOLSHED SWINGS* WITH MANY AMATURE ACTS AND KAREOKE. COME AND JOIN THE FUN".

He spotted Jimmy Woodser and Indigo Jones sitting in the shade of the *Clancy Of The Overflow* pavilion and turned to Johnny and said "Johnny, look over there, isn't that Jimmy and Indigo. I didn't expect to see them here?"

Johnny turned and said "I'm not surprised to see him here. *Australia is his name.* Come on everyone, let's go and see if he's going to tell a story."

The family group stood near Jimmy, while Jimmy looked around the gathering crowd of people, he made eye contact with Duncan and while still looking at him said *"There's no place on earth like Australia,* even *old man drought* or *when the rain tumbles down in July,* can not change the way people feel about it. The *Ghosts of the Golden Mile* still ride the *Glory Bound train* to answer a *traveller's prayer.*

You have found the one who left *on the night train* and *the angel of Goulburn Hill*; together you will make *the old rugged cross* shine and *the old rusty bell* ring out *the Shearing Song.*

57

Australia's on the wallaby for not much longer and you will no longer have to be *crying on each other's shoulder* because your *dieseline dreams* will help you *pack up your troubles* that you have within yourself and you will listen to *the whispering bush* that is in there too.

You will stop having the *road train blues* along the *road of loneliness* and be a *rover no more*. I always take notice of the little *things I see around me*, for they can help me understand what life is about." Jimmy smiled at Duncan and said no more.

Beth looked at Duncan and said "I don't understand one thing he said, but it seemed that he was only talking to you. So, do you know what he meant?"

"Yes." said Duncan, "I think I do, but it's complicated and now is not the right time for me to try and explain it to you."

He bent down and said to Jack and Angela "Let's go and have some fun."

Johnny pulled Duncan to one side out of earshot of the rest of the group and said "You can tell me what Jimmy said to you tomorrow because while he was talking, I saw Texas Jack and went and told him about the letter you received in the *morning mail* today. I also told him that you were staying with me until after Christmas, so he knows how to contact you if he needs to. He always knows how to reach me no matter where I am."

They wandered around the showground, stopping occasionally to *listen to a country song*, like the *Claypan Boogie* being played by a young group called *High, Wide and Handsome* or *the lame fiddler* playing the *Lonesome Fiddle Blues*. They had something to eat from *The Mad Cook* bake house that was joined to *a pub with no beer* that only sold soft drinks, tea and coffee.

There were also some Carnival rides set up for people to enjoy.

"The *lights on the hill* will be switched on *when the moon across the bushland beams*." Duncan heard someone say.

Angela looked at Duncan's face and said "It means that the *lights on the hill* will be switched on when it gets dark."

"Well." said Duncan "I'm just in the mood for *losin' my blues tonight*

58

because I'm having a great day and I'm still on a *natural high* from last night.

Tomorrow, we'll be *waltzing Matilda* down the road again, that's the name of Johnny's van, so will you all join me for a few more hours of fun."

Everyone laughed at what Duncan had just said. They walked past the *Man From Iron Bark* pavilion, where the teenagers were already having a good time, to the family pavilion where they could all be together.

Behind where they were sitting, Duncan heard *Kelly's offsider* talking about the heavy weight fight between *King Bundawaal* and the *King of Kalgoorlie*, and that the title went to *King Bundawaal*.

Beth moved closer to her husband and said "I feel like there's *only the two of us here* tonight. Listen to that, *our wedding waltz*, let's dance, please."

The evening flew by so quickly and soon it was time for goodbyes.

"*That's a sad affair* for both of you. You have both just found each other and now you both have to go your own separate ways after being apart for *so long.*" said Beth's husband.

Johnny said "Maybe for a few months more, Duncan will have to travel *on my road* but up until Christmas, no one knows what's going to happen.

Now we have your address Beth, we'll be able to keep you informed on Duncan's progress."

They all said good night but not good bye as they went their respective ways.

SURPRISE ENDING

Duncan sat on the side of his bed looking at the envelope addressed "*To Whom It May Concern*". Many questions started running through his head, like how did Johnny know so much? Jimmy's appearance and his story for him yesterday, the letter he was holding with the news about his sister and the coincidental and informal meeting that happened between them.

This was not a question of *what happens when a boy from Alabama meets a girl from Gundagai*, this was meeting his sister. He knew that *bye and bye* the questions would be answered.

Johnny called out "Stop your day *dreamin'* in there. I'll be waiting at the *end of the pub* down on the road for you and I want to be *on the move* in half an hour at the most. I'm going back again to Yarrawonga, *my journey home* is only a day or two away and I can't wait to get back to *my old Aussie homestead, my home on the sunburnt plains.* I don't really want to be *pushin' time along the road to Gundagai.*"

Just as Duncan was about to say goodbye to Annie, he heard her say to someone in the other room "Be careful with *my old china plate*, it's the only one I have left so don't break it."

They stopped at the showground where people were either getting ready to leave or were already leaving. Johnny said "You wait here while I go find those *old bush mates of mine.*"

Duncan heard *Kelly's offsider* yell out to the *Middleton's rouseabout* "*Send 'er down Hughie*, OK, got it. Now *send 'er down Hughie*, that should be the last. Tie them down tight or they'll be *rolling down the road.*"

"*G'day blue.*" Duncan turned to see Scobie standing behind him and thought "How did that *old feller* sneak up on me so quietly?"

"Sorry, didn't mean to startle you." said Scobie "I just came by to see *old mates* before they head off. You seemed to be on a *natural high*, did you enjoy your time here?"

"The past week has been great and full of surprises. Besides the things I've learnt from Harry and the boys, I have also met the sister, I didn't know I had and her family.

The biggest disappointment that I have now is that now I have met my sister, I don't know when or if I will see her again." said Duncan.

Scobie looked Duncan in the eyes and said "Your *crying time* has ended. *I've been there* with *Ironbark Jim*, who lives down near Johnny. He once told me to just *keep on rolling* with the flow for the *nature of man* is to start worrying when times get tough.

Never mind what other people say negatively, *steppin' around* the negativity to the positive can be the *last thing to learn* in life. Jimmy told you to listen to *the whispering bush* as it will never give you the wrong message."

Scobie saw Johnny coming and said "Ah! Johnny, I've come to say have a safe trip on *the home run* down to the *road to Gundagai* and don't go *pushin' time* too hard or you'll get the *highway fever. You know what I mean*. Well, now it's time for me to be heading off to *my happy valley home, my sunset home* where I belong and *where I'd sooner be."*

"She'll be right mate. I'm not *losing my blues tonight* over a *cattle camp reverie* by a *cattle camp crooner* or any other *camp reverie*. Don't forget that I lost *my pal alcohol*, the *whiskey blues* and the *highway fever* in the *lights on the hill* near *Sassafras Gap* while going back to *that old bush shanty of mine*.

Come on Duncan, it's time we hit the road and start *waltzing Matilda* again. You've got a story to tell me while we're travelling."

Johnny took the first stint at driving, leaving Duncan to look at the changing countryside and mull over all that was in his mind. The *trouble* was; he had so much going on in his head, that trying to sort it out only confused him more.

Since he had met Johnny, whom he found to be a *truthful fella*, while resting *there on the side of the road* heading south, his whole life has been changing in so many ways. The people he has met, subtly giving him advice, and teaching him station hand work and to top it all off, the letter from his grandparents and finding out and meeting his sister, the one who he had never known about.

Johnny gave him a sideways glance and said "There are *some things a man can't fight* and somewhere else in the world, *somebody's mother tonight* will be telling their son the same thing. Now are you going to tell me what Jimmy said to you yesterday?"

61

Duncan began with "Jimmy, *Australia is his name*, isn't it? The way I understand the meaning of what he said is, *when the rain tumbles down in July*, the *Willy Willy* that blows cold and *old man drought* means flood, the *winter wind* and drought. No matter what the weather brings, the people on the land still keep going and they stick together, keeping *country livin'* a viable prospect.

When he mentioned the Ghosts riding the *Glory Bound Train* to answer a *traveller's prayer*, I think he meant something like when you came along and picked me up, because I was at the stage where I couldn't *walk a country mile* or even a couple more steps.

He mentioned finding Beth and her family and the old rugged cross and the old rusty bell ringing, I think that meant that now I have more reasons to keep the faith because the government will grant me a work visa, so I can stay awhile longer to get to know my family and maybe settle down.

When he mentioned the bush whispering, I think he meant that I should take notice of any gut feelings I have and of *things I see around me*. I was still surprised to see him."

Johnny's reply was "Jimmy does live on *a land he calls his own*, but he is not *a prouder man than you*, in fact, he is more *the ocker* that you meet in real life and he is one of those people who will only drink in *a pub with no beer*, no matter where he is.

He once came across a *dying stockman* and dragged him on a stretcher that he had made, for two days back to a homestead on *the Birdsville Track* end of the *Nulla Creek*. He really is a *nature's gentleman* but he is treated like a *second class, wait here* person. He *never was at all* thanked for helping the stockman. Even as a bushranger, *Ned Kelly was a gentleman* and he *never was at all* treated like a *second class, wait here* person, yet he was still treated differently to Jimmy. *The only way we can change the world* is to acknowledge that everyone is different and treat all people with the respect that they deserve.

Where is country? It is *where country is*. It is the *wild rugged land that I love*, it's the *dust from the land I love*, it's *when the rain tumbles down in July*, it's *when the Currawongs come down*, it is the *ballad of the drover*, the *Claypan Boogie*, and it's the people and knowing that *we've done us proud* and much, much more.

It's *what I am to a mate* and *what I am* to myself and when I sing *my final song*; it's what the good stuff on the *tracks I left behind* me is.

You can be a *happy drover* riding *along the road of song* or the *worst in the world, bye and bye* we'll all have to ride the *Glory Bound Train* to the *range of glory. That'll do me* for now. *That's the way I am* and that's the way I think.

Oh good, here's the road I want to turn into, it'll take us to *the road to Gundagai*. When we reach Gundagai, I want to say g'day *to a mate* and we'll have a break. You can drive for a while after that."

Driving along the unsealed part of the road reminded Duncan of the time they drove *up the old Nulla road* and it was about twenty miles further down the road before they reached the sealed part of *the road to Gundagai* again.

Six miles this side of Gundagai, Johnny started laughing and Duncan asked what he was laughing at and Johnny said "Remember Scobie telling us about his dog and he buried it *where the dog sits on the tucker box,* well it's coming up and I never told Scobie that it *was the dog who stole my hat* many years earlier."

Both men were so glad to reach Gundagai where they could stretch their legs as it had been a long trip from Tamworth where they had spent the past week walking everywhere. As they walked into the roadhouse diner, Duncan heard "That's *the answer to the silvery moonlight trail.* Now are there anymore questions you want me to try and answer?"

"*Bloody bonzer mate,* I told Fred that you would know." came the reply.

Johnny walked over to talk to his mate who was serving a customer "*Must've been a hell of a party.* I don't have any White OX."

"Yeah it was, Give me a pouch of Drum then, *I must have good terbaccy when I smoke.*" said the customer.

The break was good and as Duncan was driving out of town, he saw two *old time country halls*; one decorated for a wedding reception and thought "*Somebody's mother tonight* will be feeling a bit anxious about tomorrow. I hope that I never get the *wedding bell blues* when I have to do *our wedding waltz.*"

Johnny told Duncan where to turn off, leaving *the road to Gundagai* behind. "*You just can't miss it mate.*" he said.

While they were *swingin' along that road that leads to Henty*, Johnny asked if Duncan would like to hear another story. Duncan nodded his head 'yes' because Johnny's stories were usually good.

Johnny started "One *payday at the pub* in *Larrikins Landing*, a small town about ten miles off *the road to Gundagai*, a *rovin' gambler* from *Woolloomooloo* met *Rose of Red River Valley*.

She was sitting alone having a *sad cigarette* because she had to say to her horse *Rusty it's goodbye*. During that *Sat'day in the saddle*, her horse Rusty went lame and she had to sell him. The *rovin' gambler* told the bar attendant to *set 'em up* and took her over a drink. They talked for awhile, and then she told him "I should start *walking on my way* back home." but because it was dusk, he told her that he would walk with her.

"Can you *walk a country mile* in the dark?" she asked him.

You could *hear 'em go* walking down *Sugar Shed Lane* towards *the long road* that would take her home. With the *big moon* lighting their way, they kept walking until the *lights on the hill* of an on coming vehicle lit up something on the side of the road.

They stopped to see that it was *one truckie's epitaph* and read "*Lawson's Ghost* and *Joe Palmer's Ghost* met me here on the *Glory Bound Train*. I couldn't outrun both of them, although I did *give it a go*."

They heard the *roaring wheels* of a four wheel drive come to a stop and looked up to see her brother *Redford* parked beside her.

"We just heard from *Redwing* about Rusty and I decided to come and pick you up because with it being dark, to be walking out here alone could be dangerous especially if there's an *old dingo* anywhere near here." said her brother.

Rose of Red River climbed into the vehicle and turned to thank the gambler but he was gone.

She turned to her brother and said "He's disappeared, there's *only the two of us here,* and that *one truckie's epitaph* that we stopped to look at; it's gone too."

That was years ago when it happened and it was *written afterwards* that the *Sun Valley Rose* never left here station after that.

I think we'll spend the night in Henty."

The following day, they were on the road that early, that the *Murray moon* was setting and Johnny was driving. It wasn't long before they drove through *another town* called Culcairn and over another dry creek called *Nulla Creek*.

Duncan thought "When the *rain still tumbles down in July*, I wonder how much water flows down the creek."

He was glad that he wasn't driving because it would have been easy for him to get the *highway fever*, due to the road being so straight.

"Ah! Lavington; the pub there is definitely not *a pub with no beer*, it has seven different makes on tap and *you've gotta drink the froth to get to the beer*, that means that Albury is just down the road.

We'll drive straight through and cross the Murray River into *Wodonga* and we'll have a short break there because Yarrawonga is only a two hour drive from there.

Johnny wasn't wrong and as they drove up the driveway Johnny said "Home, *bless this house,* we're home and *now I'm easy*. Home, *I'll take mine country style* anytime."

The rest of the day was spent getting settled in and being shown around the property.

The following morning they both slept in. and about mid morning, Johnny received a phone call and looked over at Duncan and smiled as he put the receiver down.

Duncan thought "What now!"

"Come outside, there's some people I want you to meet." said Johnny.

Going out the front door, Duncan saw an *old purple* Ute and a horse truck stopping in the yard. Five men alighted from the vehicles.

One of them from the Ute, turned to the three men from the truck and said "What do you mean by *how will I go with him mate*, you've handled horses like him before, just *leave him in the long yard.*" then turned back and greeted Johnny and said "He's a bit frisky, he's been up in *Rocky's run* for the past two days."

Johnny looked at Duncan and said "Meet *Joe Daly. Joe* is willing to teach you all facets of station work and to give you a job. As soon as you get your truck license, you'll be *hauling for the Double "T"* Company. He was also going to sponsor you if you needed it for the immigration mob. You will be starting with him after Christmas but until then, you'll work here with *Ironbark Jim*.

So change those *lace-up shoes* for some work boots and start working on getting some *dinkum bushman's hands*.

Next week, you will have been in Australia for ten months and as you put in your application for residency five weeks after arriving, you will be granted full residency after your eight months from processing time is up. You will soon be a *dinki di Aussie*, well almost, and you will need these."

Johnny tossed a set of keys at Duncan and continued saying "You'll need somewhere to stay when you're up north, they are the keys to *my old Cooloolah home*; it's yours now. We'll do the paper work later this arvo."

Duncan stood there flabbergasted and all he could say was "*Fair dinkum*! Thank you."

A young boy ran past Johnny and said "*I'm gonna take my dog for a run* through the *Mitchell grass. Paddy Gramp*, some of the stock hands and me will be spending *Sat'day in the saddle*."

Johnny said "To Paddy Gramp, *the saddle is his home* and always will be."

As he stood there watching the boy and his dog disappear behind a shed, he thought "All those different people who have helped me in one way or another, are they trying to *paralyse my mind?*"

That night, his mother once again came to him in a dream, looking so beautiful, happy and peaceful. When she spoke to him, her voice was so soft and tender, "*If Jesus called on you* and told you that all the people who have helped you along your journey, were *angels in disguise*, would you believe him?

Johnny is a very special person and your niece really is *the angel of Goulburn Hill* but no- one knows, and never will, except you, but you will never be able to tell them.

Life is like a river, you never know where it will take you. *Are the good days gone forever?* For you, no, they're only starting.

Any old time that you get those *lonely lonesome blues, my moonlight trail* to you will bring you *my sweetest lullaby* to let you know that *that's the song we're singing* just for you.

You've got the cleanest mind of most men and you will go far. Now it's *my time* to leave you, but remember I'll always love you and watch over you. Sleep in peace."

When he woke in the morning, Duncan went looking for Johnny to tell him about his dream, but couldn't find him anywhere. He asked other farm and stock hands if they had seen Johnny, and they all said that they had seen him heading towards his van.

Duncan hurried over to the van and found a note attached to it.

The note read "To *The New Australian Stockman, Me and Matilda* have travelled many miles together, but now is *my time* to join *my people* in *my Aussie home where the blue gums turn red in the sunset* and *the bell's of St Mary's* will be *the calling* for *the dying stockman* to join me in *my final song.*

Matilda no more is mine, I give her to you. Remember to always look after her and she will never fail you, no matter where you go or how ever far you travel in her. She has many, many, many years of travelling left in her and you will never again have to walk a country mile or ask anyone *"May I sleep in your barn tonight, mister?"*

Give my love to your sister Beth and her family, and her new baby boy will look like you. We may meet again but always remember the journey that you had to go through to get to where you are now. There is never a *last thing to learn* because you learn things every day that you are alive. Bye. Johnny."

The same young boy who had taken his dog for a run the day before, walked up to Duncan and said "Johnny's gone again, hasn't he? Will you tell me a story from your journey with him?

Duncan nodded yes with his head as he looked across to the *yellow old bullcatcher* and noticed that all the rust had gone and it looked brand new again.

He thought "I bet Beth didn't know that she's pregnant again. This is *where I'd sooner be, spending my life in the sun* and *when the rain tumbles down in July*, I'll still be happy because this is *where country is.*

No more *ramblin' shoes* or *itching feet.* Jimmy was right when he said that *there's no place on earth like Australia* 'cos *my heart's in Australia now.*"

Duncan walked away from the van with the young boy while putting Johnny's note in his pocket and yelling out to a stock hand *"Leave him in the long yard."*

Then he turned to the boy and said "Now *about this hat.*"

REFERENCE

AUSSIE SING SONG
THE ROAD TO GUNDAGAI
I'M GOING BACK AGAIN TO YARRAWONGA
THE MAN FROM THE NEVER NEVER
THAT OLD BUSH SHANTY OF MINE
CLICK GOES THE SHEARS
THE OVERLANDER TRAIL
WALTZING MATILDA
A PUB WITH NO BEER
GOODBYE MELBOURNE TOWN
BOTONY BAY
ROVER NO MORE
OH, SYDNEY I LOVE YOU
BACK TO CROAJINGALONG
BEER BARREL POLKA
THE BELLS OF ST MARY'S
TIE ME KANGAROO DOWN SPORT
WHERE THE DOG SITS ON THE TUCKER BOX
KEEP THE HOMEFIRES BURNING
PACK UP YOUR TROUBLES
A BROWN SLOUCH HAT
IT'S A LONG WAY TO TIPPERARRY
THE ANSWER TO THE PUB WITH NO BEER
THE WHISPERING BUSH
LITTLE BOY LOST
SUVLA BAY
BLESS THIS HOUSE
THE OLD SUNDOWNER
THE SILVER IN MY MOTHER'S HAIR
NOW IS THE HOUR

SONGS IN THE SADDLE
THE MAN FROM THE NEVER NEVER
WHEN THEY MUSTER ON THE GOLDEN PLAIN
THE RODEO DANCE
HARRY THE BREAKER
SAT'DAY IN THE SADDLE
SPRINGTIME ON THE RANGE
ONCE WHEN I WAS MUSTERING
THE SADDLE IS HIS HOME
MY PONY WHIPSTICK

SADDLE BOY
JUST SADDLE OLD DARKY
MAREEBA'S RODEO SONG

PEOPLE AND PLACES
SONG OF MACLEAY
DOWN AT CHARLEY GRAY'S
KEELA VALLEY
THE OLD WOOLSHED DO
MIDDLETON'S ROUSEABOUT
GAME AS NED KELLY
THE LAND OF LOTS OF TIME
OLD BUSH MATES OF MINE
MAD JACK'S COCKATOO
SWEENY
COSY INN
CHARLEY GRAY'S BARN DANCE

ANOTHER AUSSIE SING SONG
MURRUMBIDGEE ROSE
WODONGA
WHERE'S THE OLD COBBER OF MINE?
I'M LONESOME FOR SYDNEY TONIGHT
MURRAY MOON
BEAUTIFUL QUEENSLAND
OUR WEDDING WALTZ
THE OLD BULLOCK DRAY
THE SNAKE GULLY SWAGGER
GAME AS NED KELLY
WOOLLOOMOOLOO
MY HOME ON THE SUNBURNT PLAINS
DYING THE STOCKMAN
I'M GONNA HUMP MY BLUEY
BOLD TOMMY PAYNE
SWINGIN' ALONG THAT ROAD THAT LEADS TO HENTY
SNOWY RIVER
ON THE ROAD TO ANYWHERE
WHEN A BOY FROM ALABAMA MEETS A GIRL FROM
GUNDAGAI
A LITTLE BOY CALLED SMILEY
A TOWN LIKE ALICE
A SEQUEL TO THE PUB WITH NO BEER
WHERE THE BLUE GUMS TURN RED IN THE SUNSET

70

BUSHWACKER
GIVE MY LOVE TO SYDNEY TOWN
NEVER NEVER
EUMERELLA SHORE
WILD COLONIAL BOY
I'VE GOT A POSSIE WAY BACK IN AUSSIE
OUT OF THE BLUE GUMS

THE NATURE OF MAN
HIGH WIDE AND HANDSOME
WHEN YOU'RE SHORT OF A SMOKE
KEEP THE LOVELIGHT SHINING
HOW WILL I GO WITH HIM, MATE?
LOVE'S A GAME OF LET'S PRETEND
TO A MATE
I LOVE YOU BEST OF ALL
WHEN YOU'RE SHORT OF A QUID
OLD LOVE LETTERS
THE NATURE OF MAN
OUR WEDDING WALTZ
I MUST HAVE GOOD TERBACCY WHEN I SMOKE

AN EVENING WITH SLIM AND JOY
THE WILD LIFE YOU LEAD
WHEN IT'S LAMPLIGHTING TIME IN THE VALLEY
THE SPINNING WHEEL
ROAD OF LONELINESS
OLD PAINT
DOWN THE DUSTY ROAD TO HOME
ROAD TRAIN BLUES
BARB'RY ALLEN
MY LOVE'S A STRANGER NOW
IF JESUS CALLED ON YOU
BURY ME BENEATH THE WILLOW
MORNING MAIL

SONGS MY FATHER SANG TO ME
GRANNY'S HIELAND HAME
OLD LOVE LETTERS
JANE O'HARA
THE OLD LANTERN WALTZ
THE SHIP THAT NEVER RETURNED
AN OLD FASHIONED LOCKET

IT TAKES AN IRISH HEART
WHEN THE HARVEST DAYS ARE OVER
JESSIE DEAR
MY OLD KENTUCKY HOME
MY OLD PAL
TWO LITTLE GIRLS IN BLUE
GIRL I LEFT BEHIND

SONGS FROM THE CATTLE CAMP
FAIR ENOUGH
DREAM TIME VOICES
THE CROW
GHOSTS OF THE GOLDEN MILE
BACK IN THE SADDLE
I MUST HAVE GOOD TERBACCY WHEN I SMOKE
HARD HARD COUNTRY
ST PETER
OLD MAN DROUGHT
BACK WHERE I BELONG
OLD BEAU
OLD MATES

SING ALONG WITH DAD
SING ALONG WITH DAD
SAD CIGARETTE
YOU CAN'T TELL ME A THING
BEEN A FOOL TOO LONG
FRANKIE AND JOHNNY
STEPPIN' ROUND AUSTRALIA
DEAR OLD SUNNY SOUTH BY THE SEA
ANGELS IN DISGUISE
MISSOURI WALTZ
DARK DEPTHS OF THE BLUE
SIDE BY SIDE
THE OLD RUGGED CROSS

CATTLE CAMP CROONER
ARCADIA VALLEY
DRY WEATHER WIND
GETTING AWAY FROM IT ALL
CASEY'S LUCK
OLD TIBOOB'RA
SOMEWHERE UP IN QUEENSLAND

CATTLE CAMP CROONER
RIBS COOKED ON THE COALS
RELICS OF THE PAST
PADDY GRAMP
HORSE AND HOBBLE DAYS
THE WAVE HILL TRACK

SLIM DUSTY ENCORES
MY OLD AUSSIE HOMESTEAD
YOU STEPPED OUT OF LINE
THE PAPER BOY
OLD HOME WEEK
YOU'VE GOT THE CLEANEST MIND
FAIR DINKUM
PASTURES OF HOME
DREAMIN' ON THE SLIPRAIL
THAT'S A SAD AFFAIR
LONELY LOMESOME BLUES
THE WHISPERING BUSH
WHERE THE WESTERN CLOUDS AT SUNSET TURN TO GOLD

SING A HAPPY SONG
SING A HAPPY SONG
IF YOU FALL OUT OF LOVE WITH ME
BIG BEGGIN' FOOL
SET 'EM UP
STEP DOWN FROM THIS MOUNTAIN
I'M LAYIN' IT ON THE LINE
PARALYSE MY MIND
HE DON'T DESERVE YOU ANYMORE
I AIN'T A-GONNA BE TREATED THIS-A-WAY
CINDERELLA
SUGAR SHED LANE
HELLO TROUBLE

FOOLIN' AROUND
FOOLIN' AROUND
CAUSE I HAVE YOU
TOP OF THE WORLD
A PROUDER MAN THAN YOU
THIS SONG IS JUST FOR YOU
ETERNAL LOVE
GOD'S OWN SINGER OF SONGS

MANY MOTHERS
THE KINGDOM I CALL HOME
HAPPY ANNIVERSARY
THE DAY I MARRIED YOU
THE LONG ROAD

GLORY BOUND TRAIN
GLORY BOUND TRAIN
TEN GOLDEN RULES
BYE AND BYE
CALVARY HILL
WINGIN' MY WAY BACK HOME
THAT'S THE KIND OF RELIGION FOR ME
PRECIOUS LORD
WHAT THE MAN SAID
JOYBELLS IN YOUR HEART
IT'S WORTH IT
THE SOFTEST TOUCH IN TOWN
HEAVEN COUNTRY STYLE

SONGS FROM THE LAND I LOVE
WHEN THE SCRUBBERS BREAK
THE ROAD IS STILL MY HOME
THE DROVER'S COOK
LAND OF NO SECOND CHANCE
THE RETIRED DROVER
AUSTRALIAN BUSHMEN
WHEN SNOWY SINGS OF HOME
BIG JOHN
MEN WHO COME BEHIND
DUST FROM THE LAND I LOVE
CAMOOWEAL
WILLY WILLY

LIVE AT WAGGA WAGGA
GOOD OLD COUNTRY STYLE
SWEENY
THE DROVER'S COOK
GUM TREES BY THE ROADWAY
WHEN THE RAIN TUMBLES DOWN IN JULY
SOMEWHERE BETWEEN
A PUB WITH NO BEER
L.A. INTERNATIONAL AIRPORT

74

HOW WILL I GO WITH HIM, MATE?
NED KELLY WAS A GENTLEMAN
IF I ONLY HAD A HOME SWEET HOME
BYE AND BYE
HE'S JUST THE ONE
OLD TIME MUSIC

ME AND MY GUITAR
RAMBLIN' SHOES
THE MAN FROM SNOWY RIVER
"SECOND CLASS, WAIT HERE"
THAT WAS YEARS AGO
SHE WASN'T THERE TO MEET ME
MACKENZIE COUNTRY
BOOTS OF MANY COLOUR
ANTHILL STYLE
PETER ANDERSON AND CO.
DO YOU THINK THAT I DO NOT KNOW
ROUGHRIDERS
THE BIRDSVILLE TRACK
DROUGHT

LIVE AT TAMWORTH
PICKIN' AND SINGIN'
OLDTIME DROVER'S LAMENT
OLD GIDGEE TREE
ELECTION DAY
IF I WERE FREE
COUNTRY LIVIN'
LOUISIANA MAN
CUNNAMULLA FELLA
END OF THE PUB
A PICTURE OF HOME
BANKS OF THE OHIO
MIDDLETONS ROUSEABOUT
KELLY'S OFFSIDER
LIGHTS ON THE HILL
MY CLINCH MOUNTAIN HOME
GLORY BOUND TRAIN

DUSTY TRACKS
LEANING POST
ARAJOEL WALTZ
SWEET TALKING

DON'T LAUGH IN THE FACE OF FATHER TIME
WHEN THE MOON ACROSS THE BUSHLAND BEAMS
I DON'T WANT NO WOMAN AROUND
WAGON TRAINS NORTH
WEDDING BELL BLUES
A FRIEND INDEED
THE HAPPIEST DAYS OF ALL
SLOW DOWN
THE BOYS WHO NEVER RETURNED

TALL STORIES AND SAD SONGS
BELIEVE IT OR NOT
THE JIMBERELLA KID
THE DOG WHO STOLE MY HAT
FROM THE GULF TO ADELAIDE
ONLY THE TWO OF US HERE
HAPPY JACK
THE MAN FROM IRON BARK
THE HANGOVER SONG
GIVE IT A GO
I HOPE THEY FIGHT AGAIN
BALLAD OF THE DROVER
HOLYDAN
CANETOAD'S PLAIN CODE

AUSTRALIANA
GRANDFATHER JOHNSON
CLANCY OF THE OVERFLOW
THE LAME FIDDLER
A SQUATTER'S PRAYER
HENRY LAWSON
DROUGHT TIME
STICK TO HIM BLUEY
WRITTEN AFTERWARDS
THE BEQUEST
THE PUBS STILL MAKE A QUID
A DROVERS LIFE
LAST OF THE BREED

DINKI DI AUSSIE
THE DESERT LAIR
RETURN OF THE STOCKMAN
THE NEW AUSTRALIAN BUSHMAN

A ROSE OF RED
THE MAN FROM THE NEVER NEVER
LITTLE OLD ONE HORSE PUB
ROAD TRAINS
BRIGALOW BILL
DINKI DI AUSSIE
THE SADDLE IS HIS HOME
THIS CHAP KNOWS A LOT
"SO LONG, OLD MATES"

LIGHTS ON THE HILL
PUSHIN' TIME
THE HOME RUN
WORST IN THE WORLD
FOGGY MIRRORS
RIDIN' THIS ROAD
INTERSTATER
LIGHTS ON THE HILL
BENT-AXLE BOB
THERE LIES A WORKHORSE
TRUCKIN'S IN MY BLOOD
A TRUCKIE'S LAST WILL AND TESTAMENT
HEAR 'EM GO

WAY OUT THERE
WAY OUT THERE
PAY DAY AT THE PUB
SUNNY SOUTHERN SUE
FADED COAT OF BLUE
SILVER SPURS
BIG MOON
MY HOME ON THE SUNBURNT PLAINS
HIGHWAY BLUES
MY JOURNEY HOME (IT'S NEVER THE SAME)
MOTHER'S WEDDING BAND
THE DECIMAL CURRENCY PUB
SHOWERS OF BLESSINGS

THINGS I SEE AROUND ME
THINGS I SEE AROUND ME
BLACKENED QUARTS ARE BOILING
COPPED THE LOT
NOT MUCH TO SHOW

COMMERCIAL D.T.'S
HARRY BOWDEN...DERELICT
SMILES
THREE RIVERS HOTEL
END OF THE CANNING STOCK ROUTE
GOOD OLD DAYS
THE LAST OF THE BUSHMEN
THE BULL STAG

GIVE ME THE ROAD
GIVE ME THE ROAD
THE ANGEL OF GOULBURN HILL
YOU TAKE HER FROM NARRANDERA
THE BOSS MAN
WE'VE BEEN TRUCKING TOO
DANGER ROAD TRAIN
HIGHWAY ONE
ROARING THROUGH THE NIGHT
KELLY'S OFFSIDER
YOU JUST CAN'T MISS IT MATE
THE GREAT AUSTRALIAN WHINGER
ROAD TRAIN BLUES

SONGS FROM DOWN UNDER
OLD RIDERS IN THE GRANDSTAND
A CERTAIN KIND OF GOLD
LETTERS FROM DOWN UNDER
BALLAD OF HENRY LAWSON
JUST GOING HOME
ROADLINER
COBB AND CO. TWITCH
SADNESS AND I WANDER HOME
WILD RUGGED LAND THAT I LOVE
SONG OF THE WEST
WALTZING MATILDA
RODEO RIDERS

JUST SLIM WITH OLD FRIENDS
ABOUT THIS HAT
I'LL MEET HIM TOMORROW
THAT OLD BLUE DOG OF MINE
THE ROUND TABLE
GATES

OLD GILBERT
BUSH POETS OF AUSTRALIA
STOCK HORSES
JOE PALMER'S GHOST
THE DROVER'S YARN
LAWSON'S GHOST
CATCHING YELLOWBELLY (IN THE BARCOO)

ON THE MOVE
ON THE MOVE
MY TIME
INDIAN PACIFIC
FINALLY MADE IT HOME
YOU KNOW WHAT I MEAN
ANYDAY WOMAN
ISA
THE FRONT ROW
BILLY MAC
HIGHWAY BLUES
JOE (DON'T LET YOUR MUSIC KILL YOU)
WHAT AM I DOING IN THIS TOWN

TRAVELLIN' COUNTRY MAN
TRAVELLIN' COUNTRY BAND
GOD'S OWN SINGER OF SONGS
ALTHEA
SADNESS AND I WANDERED HOME
SPANISH PIPE DREAM
IF THOSE LIPS COULD ONLY SPEAK
THE ROSE IN HER HAIR
STREETS OF SYDNEY
JESUS TAKES A HOLD
BIG TIME (JUST BECAUSE YOU'RE IN DEEP ELEM)
FOOLIN' AROUND
I BROKE A PROMISE
I HEARD THE BLUEBIRD SING
LIFE IS LIKE A RIVER

TO WHOM IT MAY CONCERN
TO WHOM IT MAY CONCERN
BEAT OF THE GOVERNMENT STROKE
OLD BUSH BARBEQUE
A LETTER FROM ARRABURY

5 am BLUES
AND THE BAND PLAYED WALTZING MATILDA
HIGHWAY FEVER
MARTY
42 TYRES
SOME THINGS A MAN CAN'T FIGHT
IRONBARK JIM
MAN IN THE GLASS

THE ENTERTAINER
TRAVELLIN' COUNTRY BAND
PICKIN' AND SINGIN'
ABOUT THIS HAT
PUSHIN'TIME
MOVIN' ON
WHEN IT'S LAMPLIGHTING TIME IN THE VALLEY
RED RIVER VALLEY
KELLY'S OFFSIDER
WALK RIGHT IN
I MUST HAVE GOOD TERBACCY WHEN I SMOKE
WHEN THE RAIN TUMBLES DOWN IN JULY
MIDDLETON'S ROUSEABOUT
TRUMBY
DROVER'S COOK
A PUB WITH NO BEER
FRONT ROW
THREE RIVERS HOTEL
INDIAN PACIFIC
THE ROAD TO GUNDAGAI
JAMBALAYA
I FALL TO PIECES
LISTEN TO A COUNTRY SONG
CRAZY
OH LONESOME ME
SUNSET YEARS OF LIFE
CAMOOWEAL
CATCHING YELLOWBELLY (IN THE BARCOO)
LEAD ME DOWN TO THE STOCKYARD
COUNTRY LIVIN'
CLOSEST THING TO FREEDOM
THE ANGEL OF GOULBURN HILL
THE BIGGEST DISAPPOINTMENT
LIGHTS ON THE HILL

GLORY BOUND TRAIN

RARITIES
SONG FOR THE AUSSIES
MY FINAL SONG
YOUR BEST PAL IS MOTHER
MY SWEETEST LULLABY
BORN TO BE A YODELLER
HEADING FOR THAT BRUMBY TRAIL
THE SOLDIER'S WIFE
BABY OF MY DREAMS
LOVER'S LAMENT
HAPPY DROVER

SPIRIT OF AUSTRALIA
SPIRIT OF AUSTRALIA
NINETEEN EIGHTIES BUSHMAN ON THE MOVE
OLD IVENHOE
JOE MAGUIRE'S PUB
DROVING BY TRAIN
WHILE THE DAMPER COOKS
GIVE IT A GO, MATE
HARRY AND THE BREAKER
MOUNTAIN MAN'S GIRL
FAMILY OF MAN
WESTWARD HO!
LOSIN' MY BLUES TONIGHT

RODEO RIDERS
ROUGH RIDERS
OLD RIDERS IN THE GRANDSTAND
MAREEBA'S RODEO SONG
ROPE AND SADDLE BLUES
RODEO RIDERS
NOT MUCH TO SHOW
CATTLE CAMP REVERIE
THE BATTLE WITH THE ROAN
STOCK HORSES
THE ISA RODEO
HOW WILL I GO WITH HIM, MATE?
WHOA BULLOCKS WHOA
WALK A COUNTRY MILE

A COUNTRY MILE
SON OF NOISY DAN
WHEN THE RAIN TUMBLES DOWN IN JULY
JOHNNY FOSTER (THE OLD TIME TRAVELLING SHOWMAN)
MUSIC MY DAD PLAYED TO ME
OLD STOCK RIDIN' DAYS
D TOWARDS THE HEAD
THE DAY I WENT BACK HOME
SEND 'ER DOWN HUGHIE
A PUB WITH NO BEER
MANY YESTERDAYS AGO
OLD BUSH MATES OF MINE
TERRITORY RINGER
IN MY HOUR OF DARKNESS

THE MAN WHO STEADIES THE LEAD
THE MAN WHO STEADIES THE LEAD
LEAVE HIM IN THE LONG YARD
DREAMIN'
THE FOXLEIGH RODEO
NOW I'M EASY
AN INDEPENDENT BLOKE
THE BALLAD OF BIG BILL SMITH
NO MAN'S LANDPLAINS OF PEPPIMENARTI
THE CLEARING SALE
FOOLSCAP TOMBSTONES
GIVE MY REGARDS TO EDNA
THE PEARL OF THEM ALL

THE SLIM DUSTY FAMILY ALBUM
WHAT I AM
OLD TIME CHRISTMAS
TROUBLE
LOCAL MARY MAGDALEN
MEMORIES
COUNTRY REVIVAL
COUNTRY MUSIC'S IN OUR BONES
MY OLD CHINA PLATE
OLD SUNLANDER VAN
FEELING SORRY FOR ME
RODEO CLOWN
WIND UP GRAMOPHONE
NOBODY HEARD

NO 50 GOLDEN ANNIVERSARY
COUNTRY REVIVAL
LEAVE HIM IN THE LONG YARD
A PUB WITH NO BEER
WALK A COUNTRY MILE
CAMOOWEAL
INDIAN PACIFIC
HIGHWAY FEVER
THE MAN FROM SNOWY RIVER
LIGHTS ON THE HILL
THREE RIVERS HOTEL
BEAT OF THE GOVERNMENT STROKE
I DON'T SLEEP AT NIGHT
WHEN THE RAIN TUMBLES DOWN IN JULY
THE ANGEL OF GOULBURN HILL
KELLY'S OFFSIDER
THINGS I SEE AROUND ME
THE BIGGEST DISAPPOINTMENT
DUNCAN

WHERE COUNTRY IS
G'DAY BLUE
DINKUM BUSHMAN'S HANDS
WHERE COUNTRY IS
THE BIG WET IS OVER
MACK – A FINAL TRIBUTE
NO PLACE ON EARTH LIKE AUSTRALIA
ONE TRUCKIE'S EPITAPH
THE BOGONG
THE OCKER
INIGO JONES – INDIGO JONES
REDFORD
BIG YABBIES FROM THE CREEK

WHO'S RIDING OLD HARLEQUIN NOW?
WHO'S RIDING OLD HARLEQUIN NOW?
NULLA CREEK
EVERY LITTLE BIT OF AUSTRALIA
OLD DAN
THE BRASS WELL
YOU'RE COUNTRY'S BEEN SOLD
BANJO'S MAN
OLD KING COAL

LAST THING TO LEARN
I GUESS YOU HAVE
CAPTAIN THUNDERBOLT
IT TAKES A DROUGHT

ON THE WALLABY
AUSTRALIA'S ON THE WALLABY
ANOTHER DAY
ANOTHER TOWN
ROCKY'S RUN
WATER – IF IT TOOK FIFTY YEARS
OLD FELLER
ARE THE GOOD DAYS GONE FOREVER
OLD TIME COUNTRY HALLS
TWO RATS OF TOBRUK
SO MANY BALLADS TO PLAY
DUST AND SADDLE GREASE
GETTING' UP AND GOIN', SONNY

I HAVEN'T CHANGED A BIT
AUSTRALIA IS HIS NAME
COMING DOWN THE BARKLY
CALLAGHAN'S HOTEL
THE PUB ROCK
DROWNIN' MY BLUES
LIFE IS LIKE A RIVER
DON'T FOOL AROUND ANYMORE
THE BALLAD OF PORT MACQUARIE
AUSSIE DOGHOUSE BLUES
THE MELBOURNE CUP
I HAVEN'T CHANGED A BIT
THIS COUNTRY OF MINE
GOLDRUSH COUNTRY
NEVER MIND

TRUCKS ON THE TRACK
THREE HUNDRED HORSES
LONG BLACK ROAD
I'M MARRIED TO MY BULLDOG MACK
TRUCKS ON THE TRACK
FROM HERE TO THERE AND BACK
DRIBBLER BILL
DIESELINE DREAMS

FILL 'ER UP
HOME COOKIN'
TRUCKS
TARPS AND TRAILERS
DOGS
DUST AND DIESEL
THAT'S NOT ME

THE SLIM DUSTY MOVIE
THE MAN WITH THE HAT TURNED DOWN IN FRONT
COUNTRY REVIVAL
THE ISA RODEO
ROUGH RIDERS
CUNNAMULLA FELLA
ISA
JUST ROLLIN
CORROBOREE SEQUENCE
PLAINS OF PEPPIMENARTI
HOW WILL I GO WITH HIM, MATE?
PUSHIN' TIME
A PUB WITH NO BEER
CAMOOWEAL
INDIAN PACIFIC
ARE THE GOOD DAYS GONE FOREVER?
GUMTREES BY THE ROADWAY
WHERE IS COUNTRY
SONG FOR THE AUSSIES
OLD SUNLANDER VAN
WALK A COUNTRY MILE
WIND UP GRAMOPHONE
TROUBLE
LOSIN' MY BLUES TONIGHT
ONLY THE TWO OF US HERE
OLD FELLER
MY FINAL SONG
WHEN THE RAIN TUMBLES DOWN IN JULY
BACK TO MY OLD NORTHERN HOME
OLD TIME COUNTRY HALLS
THE BIGGEST DISAPPOINTMENT
LIGHTS ON THE HILL
GYMKHANA YODEL
STAY AWAY FROM ME
KEEP THE LOVELIGHT SHINING

I'LL TAKE MINE COUNTRY STYLE
CUNNAMULLA FELLER
DADDY'S GIRL
CHRISTMAS AT THE STATION
YOU'D BETTER BE WAITING
I'LL TAKE MINE COUNTRY STYLE
THE DRUNKARD
MY PAL ALCOHOL
THE ROAD TO GUNDAGAI
THE ACE OF HEARTS
IF YOU WALK OUT THAT GATE
MAPLE SUGAR SWEETHEART
WHERE THE DESERT FLOWERS BLOOM
ROSE OF RED RIVER VALLEY
SOMEBODY'S MOTHER

SINGER FROM DOWN UNDER
SINGER FROM DOWN UNDER
BORN WITH AN ENDLESS THIRST
YOU'VE GOTTA DRINK THE FROTH TO GET THE BEER
MY SON'S GUITAR
THE BALLAD OF HENRY HOLLOWAY
TONIGHT THE WOOLSHED SWINGS
STRINGYBARK AND GREENHIDE
HENRY LAWSON'S PEN
THEY DRANK AND DRANK AND DRANK
I'M DUSTY ALL OVER
LIFE'S RIDE
TRAVELLERS' PRAYER

TO A MATE – SLIM DUSTY REMEMBERS "MACK"CORMACK
TO A MATE
A PICTURE OF HOME
HAPPY JACK
THE FROG
WHEN THE MOON ACROSS THE BUSHLAND BEAMS
HOW WILL I GO WITH HIM, MATE?
THAT WAS YEARS AGO
CATTLE
CAMP REVERIE
CAMOOWEAL
SO LONG
OLD MATES

GIVE IT A GO
OLD MATES
IN MY HOUR OF DARKNESS

BEER DRINKING SONGS OF AUSTRALIA
HE'S A GOOD BLOKE WHEN HE'S SOBER
YOU'VE GOT TO DRINK THE FROTH TO GET TO THE BEER
A PUB WITH NO BEER
THE HANGOVER SONG
MAD JACK'S COCKATOO
MY PAL ALCOHOL
WHISKEY BLUES
PAY DAY AT THE PUB
OLD BUSH BARBEQUE
THREE RIVERS HOTEL
THE BOXING KANGAROO
BORN WITH AN ENDLESS THIRST
JOE MAGUIRE'S PUB
THE PUB ROCK
THE PUBS STILL MAKE A QUID
THE PUB THAT DOESN'T SELL BEER
THE ANSWER TO THE PUB WITH NO BEER
CALLAGHAN'S HOTEL
DUNCAN
END OF THE PUB

AUSTRALIA IS HIS NAME
TRAVELLIN' COUNTRY BAND
WHEN THE RAIN TUMBLES DOWN IN JULY
THE ROAD TO GUNDAGAI
I'M GOING BACK AGAIN TO YARRAWONGA
THE MAN FROM THE NEVER NEVER
THAT OLD BUSH SHANTY OF MINE
IRONBARK JIM
OLD BUSH BARBEQUE
SPIRIT OF AUSTRALIA
SEND 'ER DOWN HUGHIE
LIGHTS ON THE HILL
ALONG THE ROAD OF SONG
AUSTRALIA IS HIS NAME
LETTER FROM DOWN UNDER
OLD WOOLSHED DO
ISA RODEO

COBB AND CO. TWITCH
THE ANSWER TO THE PUB WITH NO BEER
SUNDOWN
THE ANGEL OF GOULBURN HILL
WALTZING MATILDA
CATTLE CAMP REVERIE
DARWIN (BIG HEART OF THE NORTH)
HORSE AND HOBBLE DAYS
LEAVE HIM IN THE LONG YARD
BANJO'S MAN
OLD TIME COUNTRY HALLS
A PUB WITH NO BEER
WILLY WILLY
OLD MAN DROUGHT
THE MELBOURNE CUP
GOOD OLD COUNTRY STYLE
WHEN THE RAIN TUMBLES DOWN IN JULY
INDIAN PACIFIC
BOOMERANG
TIE ME KANGAROO DOWN SPORT
WHERE THE DOG SITS ON THE TUCKER BOX
AUSTRALIAN BUSHMEN
CLANCY OF THE OVERFLOW
BUSH POETS OF AUSTRALIA
THINGS I SEE AROUND ME
THE DYING STOCKMAN
WALK A COUNTRY MILE
BIG FROGS IN LITTLE PUDDLES
A SEQUEL TO A PUB WITH NO BEER
TRUMBY
JOE MAGUIRE'S PUB
EVERY LITTLE BIT OF AUSTRALIA
THE BIRDSVILLE TRACK
G'DAY BLUE
THE OLD BULLOCK DRAY
THE SNAKE GULLY SWAGGER
GAME AS NED KELLY
WOOLLOOMOOLOO
FROM THE GULF TO ADELAIDE
THE BRASS WELL
HARRY THE BREAKER
WHERE IS COUNTRY

WHEN A BOY FROM ALABAMA MEETS A GIRL FROM
GUNDAGAI
A LITTLE BOY CALLED SMILEY
A TOWN LIKE ALICE
LAST THING TO LEARN
CHARLEY GRAY'S BARNDANCE
HENRY LAWSON
DIESELINE DREAMS
A PUB WITH NO BEER

LIVE ACROSS AUSTRALIA (THE SLIM DUSTY FAMILY)
LONESOME FIDDLE BLUES
KELLY'S OFFSIDER
MIDDLETON'S ROUSEABOUT
THE FRONT ROW
GIVE MY REGARDS TO EDNA
A FOOL SUCH AS I
CRYING TIME
I'M THINKING TONIGHT OF MY BLUE EYES
ORANGE BLOSSOM SPECIAL
GOOD HEARTED WOMAN
LAST TRAIN TO NOWHERE
LUXURY LINER
GYMKHANA YODEL
I NEED SOMEBODY TO HOLD ME WHEN I CRY
YODEL DOWN THE VALLEY
LEAVE HIM IN THE LONG YARD
ONE TRUCKIE'S EPITAPH
GLORY BOUND TRAIN

STORIES I WANT TO TELL
MOUNT BUKAROO
THE OLD JIMMY WOODSER
BREAK O' DAY
WHEN THE CURRAWONGS COME DOWN
I'VE SEEN HIS FACE BEFORE
THE SHEARING SONG
BIBLE OF THE BUSH
TO AN OLD MATE
TWO OLD GENTLMEN
WHY DON'T YOU JUST GO FISHING?
ANDY'S RETURN
ON THE NIGHT TRAIN

COUNTRY LIVIN'
CITY BROTHER
AH, FORGET IT
TEENAGE COUNTRY STYLE
BOOMERANG
THERE'S A RAINBOW AROUND MY MEMORIES
NIGHT WATCH BLUES
REDWING
COUNTRY LIVIN'
MY PEOPLE
MOVIN' AWAY
THE CUNNIN' ROO SHOOTER
WE'LL HAVE TO STICK TOGETHER
TINY BLUE SHOE
GOD WILL PREVAIL

CATTLEMEN FROM THE HIGH PLAINS
CATTLEMEN FROM THE HIGH PLAINS
INNAMINCKA MUSTER
AXE MARK ON A GIDGEE
BIG GULF RIVERS
A LAND HE CALLS HIS OWN
THE MAD COOK
THE BUSH HAS HAD ENOUGH
THAT'S MY KIND OF BRAND
THE ANNUAL RODEO SHOW
KEEROONGOOLOO STATION
WHEN BITUMEN REACHES POONCARIE
BULLOCK DUNG NARRATION
KING ALLIGATOR
BAKING A BROWNIE

HERITAGE ALBUM
WE'VE DONE US PROUD
GHOSTS OF THE GOLDEN MILE
GRANDFATHER JOHNSON
TONIGHT THE WOOLSHED SWINGS
NAMATJIRA
CLANCY OF THE OVERFLOW
GAME AS NED KELLY
THE BRASS WELL
KING BUNDAWAAL
THE MAN FROM SNOWY RIVER

90

THE MAN FROM IRON BARK
MIDDLETON'S ROUSEABOUT
OLD TIME COUNTRY HALLS
THE ISA RODEO
EVERY LITTLE BIT OF AUSTRALIA
WAGON TRAINS NORTH
BANJO'S MAN
WALTZING MATILDA

NEON CITY
GOTTA KEEP MOVING
MY OLD MIDNIGHT SPECIAL (AND ME)
NEON CITY
SALLY – THE GIRL ON CHANNEL 8
I'M THANKFUL
WHITE LINE
BILLINUDGEL
OLD KENTUCKY RIG
THE WORLD'S LAST TRUCK DRIVIN' MAN
OLD DINGO
BLUE PACIFIC RIG
I KNEW YOUR FATHER REAL WELL

SLIM DUSTY SINGS STAN COSTER
THREE RIVERS HOTEL
THE BIRDSVILLE TRACK
WHOA BULLOCKS WHOA
THE BATTLE WITH THE ROAN
ITCHING FEET
COBB AND CO. TWITCH
OLD RIDERS IN THE GRANDSTAND
CLAYPAN BOOGIE
CATCHING YELLOWBELLY (IN THE OLD BARCOO)
SOME THINGS A MAN CAN'T FIGHT
BY THE FIRE OF THE GIDGEE COAL
AUSTRALIAN BUSHMEN

G'DAY G'DAY
G'DAY G'DAY
GOOD OLD FEED OF FLATHEAD
CHRISTMAS, WHEN I WAS BIG AS YOU
A GIRL FROM THE LAND
I CAN STILL HEAR DAD SWEARING

BREAKAWAY
HOW'S YOUR MEMORY?
SITTING ON THE OLD FRONT VERANDA
THE JOHNSONVILLE DANCE
BLOODY BONZER MATE
THE BOSS
UP THE OLD NULLA ROAD

KING OF KALGOORLIE
ON MY ROAD
LIKE A FAMILY TO ME
KING OF KALGOORLIE
STILL THE WAY I FEEL
STRAIGHT AHEAD
THE LAST RIDE
BALLADEERS OF AUSTRALIA
CITY OF MT ISA
LADY LUCK
SANDS OF TANAM!
A THOUSAND YEARS AGO
JIM

HENRY LAWSON AND BANJO PATERSON
SWEENY
MIDDLETON'S ROUSEABOUT
BILL
A WORD TO TEXAS JACK
AS GOOD AS NEW
SINCE THEN
ST PETER
CALLAGHAN'S HOTEL
A MATE CAN DO NO WRONG
MEN WHO CAME BEHIND
"SECOND CLASS, WAIT HERE"
PETER ANDERSON & CO.
DO YOU THINK THAT I DO NOT KNOW
A PROUDER MAN THAN YOU
ONLY THE TWO OF US HERE
BALLAD OF THE DROVER
WRITTEN AFTERWARDS
THE BRASS WELL
MOUNT BUKAROO
THE OLD JIMMY WOODSER

BREAK O' DAY
TO AN OLD MATE
ANDY'S RETURN
ON THE NIGHT TRAIN
THE MAN FROM SNOWY RIVER
THE MAN FROM IRON BARK
CLANCY OF THE OVERFLOW
WALTZING MATILDA

TWO SINGERS ONE SONG
CRYING ON EACH OTHER'S SHOULDER
THERE AT THE SIDE OF THE ROAD
TWO SINGERS (ONE SONG)
MY OLD PAL
LIKE A BOOMERANG
MURRAY MOON
DROVIN'
IN MY GRANDMOTHER'S ARMS
MY FAVOURITE PEOPLE
ROCK THIS JOINT
I LOVE MY TRUCK
WE CAN CHANGE THE WORLD

COMING HOME
THE ONLY WAY
FURTHER OUT
THE FLYING DOCTOR'S BALL
GOOD HARD DOG
OLD BUSH PUB
LOGAN
SALE DAY AT ST LAWRENCE
CLARA WATERS
NARDOO BURNS
ROY
HUMPTY DOO WALTZ
DINOSUAR
WHERE I'D SOONER BE
LACE-UP SHOES
YELLOW GULLY
TEX MORTON
REGAL ZONOPHONE
THE WORLD'S BIGGEST CEDAR TREE
THE ONLY TIME A FISHERMAN TELLS THE TRUTH

THE OUTBACK'S NOT SO WAY BACK ANYMORE
NEBO PUB
CAMP COOKS
MY OLD COOLOOLAH HOME
FOOTSTEPS COMING HOME

A LAND HE CALLS HIS OWN
CATTLEMEN FROM THE HIGH PLAINS
AUSTRALIA'S ON THE WALLABY
SITTIN' ON THE OLD FRONT VERANDA
OLD KENTUCKY RIG
WHEN THE CURRAWONGS COME DOWN
HENRY LAWSON'S PEN
NULLA CREEK
THE SHEARING SONG
GRANDFATHER JOHNSON
MY SON'S GUITAR
THE CROW
MOUNT BUKAROO
THE BIRDSVILLE TRACK
HARRY THE BREAKER
THE DOG WHO STOLE MY HAT
G'DAY G'DAY
DINKUM BUSHMAN'S HANDS
SON OF NOISY DAN
HIGHWAY FEVER
SINGER FROM DOWN UNDER
CATCHING YELLOWBELLY (IN THE OLD BARCOO)
STOCK HORSES
IT TAKES A DROUGHT
HARD HARD COUNTRY
KEEROONGOOLOO STATION
DROVIN'
CAMPFIRE YARNS
WHEN SNOWY SINGS OF HOME
CAMOOWEAL
MY TIME
THE FRONT ROW
SOME THINGS A MAN CAN'T FIGHT
NO PLACE ON EARTH LIKE AUSTRALIA
PLAINS OF PEPPIMENARTI
THE FOXLEIGH RODEO
MORNING MAIL

95

TRAVELLIN' GUITAR
ROVIN' GAMBLER
BUMMING AROUND
WHISKEY BLUES
CAN I SLEEP IN YOUR BARN TONIGHT?
THREE TIMES SEVEN
LITTLE BLOSSOM
TRAVELLIN' GUITAR
DOWN THE TRACK
I'LL BE A BACHELOR TILL I DIE
SOMEBODY'S MOTHER TONIGHT
SPENDING MY LIFE IN THE SUN
WINTER WINDS
WHIPLASH

LIVE INTO THE 90s
G'DAY G'DAY
I'M GOING BACK AGAIN TO YARRAWONGA
THE FLYING DOCTOR'S BALL
THINGS ARE NOT THE SAME ON THE LAND
AUCTIONEER
LACE UP SHOES
CATCHING YELLOWBELLY (IN THE OLD BARCOO)
WHEN THE CURRAWONGS COME DOWN
AUSSIE DOGHOUSE BLUES
TO WHOM IT MAY CONCERN
BEEN A FOOL TOO LONG
THAT'LL DO ME
THREE HUNDRED HORSES
HIGH DRY AND HOMELESS
I'M STILL HERE TO GIVE IT MY BEST
YODEL MEDLEY 1) PRAIRIE LOVEKNOT
MEDLEY 2) THE VALLEY WHERE FRANGIPANIS GROW
MEDLEY 3) MY SUNSET HOME
MEDLEY 4) YODEL DOWN THE VALLEY
LIGHTS ON THE HILL
LOSIN' MY BLUES TONIGHT

THAT'S THE SONG WE'RE SINGING
THAT'S THE SONG WE'RE SINGING
JACK O'HAGAN
SHE'LL BE RIGHT, MATE
TIBROGARGAN

THAT'S THE WAY I AM
THE DAY WE SOLD THE FARM
BUCKING HORSE CALLED TIME
MANGROVE BOOGIE KINGS
MY DAD WAS A ROADTRAIN MAN
HARD AND CALLOUSED HANDS
MEMORY HOTEL
ALL MY MATES ARE GONE
LIFE BEHIND THE WINDSCREEN
THE LAST OF HER LINE
OLD BUSH ROAD

RINGER FROM THE TOP END
RINGER FROM THE TOP END
WHEN THE COUNTRY'S WET
I'VE BEEN, SEEN AND DONE THAT
WHERE I WANT TO BE
LIFE'S GETTING BETTER ALL THE TIME
DOWN AT THE WOOLSHED
GEORGINA'S SON
CHARLEVILLE
OLD RIVER GUM
YOU CAN'T TAKE AUSTRALIA FROM ME
POONCARIE
SHANTY ON THE RISE
FIDDLE MAN
BUNDA WATERHOLE
AFTER ALL

FIDDLER MAN
FIDDLER MAN (AUDIO MURPHY)

THE ANNIVERSARY ALBUM NO. 2
SONG FOR THE AUSSIES
SPIRIT OF AUSTRALIA
PLAINS OF PEPPIMENARTI
WHERE COUNTRY IS
G'DAY BLUE
NO PLACE ON EARTH LIKE AUSTRALIA
THE BRASS WELL
BANJO'S MAN
AUSTRALIA'S ON THE WALLABY
YOU'VE GOT TO DRINK THE FROTH TO GET TO THE BEER

WHY WORRY NOW
ANSWER TO THE SILVERY MOONLIGHT TRAIL
I BET YOU FEEL THE SAME
SUN VALLEY ROSE
GOOD OLD SANTA CLAUS
WHISKEY BLUES
YOU MADE ME LIVE LOVE AND DIE
THE GRANDEST HOMESTEAD OF ALL
DOLLY DIMPLE DANCE
WHEN THE SUN GOES DOWN OUTBACK
WHEN THE HARVEST DAYS ARE OVER
JESSIE DEAR
RUSTY IT'S GOODBYE
LOSIN' MY BLUES TONIGHT
ROSE OF REMEMBERANCE
THE RAIN STILL TUMBLES DOWN
WHEN I FIRST SAW THE LOVELIGHT IN YOUR EYES
I MUST HAVE GOOD TERBACCY WHEN I SMOKE
BABY OF MY DREAMS
GOLDY GIRL
THE SUNLANDER
THE SHOWMAN'S SONG
THE BUSHLAND BOOGIE
ANY OLD TIME
LOVER'S LAMENT
FRANKIE AND JOHNNY
IF I ONLY HAD A HOME SWEET HOME
THE BROKEN HOME
TAKE MY WORRIES AWAY
THE SWAGMAN'S STORY
MOTHER
OUR WEDDING WALTZ
A LITTLE GIRL DRESSED IN BLUE
OLD LOVE LETTERS
LONESOME ROAD OF TEARS
KING BUNDAWAAL
RANGE OF GLORY
RUNAWAY HEART
INTRO: OH! JOHNNY OH!
GOING TO THE BARNDANCE TONIGHT
SINCE THE BUSHLAND BOOGIE CAME THIS WAY
JUST SADDLE OLD DARKIE
THE RODEO DANCE

SUNNY NORTHERN ROSE
RUTLAND RODEO
HARRY THE BREAKER
QUEENSLAND STATE SO FAIR
WALKIN' ON MY WAY
GUMTREES BY THE ROADWAY
PASTURES OF HOME
DREAMIN' ON THE SLIP RAIL
ROARING WHEELS
THE NATURE OF MAN
SADDLE BOY
A PUB WITH NO BEER

COUNTRY WAY OF LIFE
ROCK 'N ROLL IN A COWBOY HAT
ROUGH RIDIN' RODEO
WHO WANTS MOSS?
AS THE BUSH COMES TO TOWN
MY HEART'S IN AUSTRALIA NOW
I WON'T BELIEVE IT'S NEVER GONNA RAIN
OLD ROCK 'N' ROLLER
JOE DALY
OLD WOOLSHED BALL
TOP SPRINGS
FIFTEEN HUNDERED HEAD
ME AND MATILDA
BROWN BOTTLE BLUES
COUNTRY WAY OF LIFE

THE SLIM DUSTY SHOW – LIVE IN TOWNSVILLE 1956
THE RUTLAND RODEO
HEY GOOD LOOKIN'
THE BUSHLAND BOOGIE
HONKY TONK BLUES
NO GOOD BABY
GOIN' TO THE BARN DANCE TONIGHT
A FOOL SUCH AS I
RANGE OF GLORY
I'LL BE STEPPIN' TOO
A PUB WITH NO BEER
BLACK COTTON STRAND

COUNTRY CLASSICS – SLIM DUSTY
DISC 1 1947 - 1969
WHEN THE RAIN TUMBLES DOWN IN JULY (ORIGINAL
VERSION)
MY AUSSIE HOME
SAT'DAY IN THE SADDLE
SPRINGTIME ON THE RANGE
THE GRANDEST HOMESTEAD OF ALL
WHEN THE SUN GOES DOWN OUTBACK
THE RAIN STILL TUMBLES DOWN
OUR WEDDING WALTZ
KING BUNDAWAAL
A PUB WITH NO BEER (ORIGINAL VERSION)
SADDLE BOY
ALONG THE ROAD TO GUNDAGAI
BY A FIRE OF GIDGEE COAL
SONG OF AUSTRALIA
MIDDLETON'S ROUSEABOUT
DOWN THE DUSTY ROAD TO HOME
CAMPFIRE YARN
THE OLD LANTERN WALTZ
GHOSTS OF THE GOLDEN MILE
STEPPIN' ROUND AUSTRALIA
CATTLE CAMP CROONER
DISC 2 1971 – 1979: CAMOOWEAL:
AUSTRALIAN BUSHMEN
GLORY BOUND TRAIN
THE MAN FROM SNOWY RIVER
THE BIRDSVILLE TRACK
MAN FROM IRON BARK
CLANCY OF THE OVERFLOW
HENRY LAWSON
LIGHTS ON THE HILL
THE THINGS I SEE AROUND ME
THREE RIVERS HOTEL
KELLY'S OFFSIDER
BUSH POETS OF AUSTRALIA
INDIAN PACIFIC
ISA
SPIRIT OF AUSTRALIA
LOSIN' MY BLUES TONIGHT
WALK A COUNTRY MILE
WHEN THE RAIN TUMBLES DOWN IN JULY

A PUB WITH NO BEER
DISC 3 1980 – 1995
DUNCAN
LEAVE HIM IN THE LONG YARD
PLAINS OF PEPPIMENARTI
COUNTRY REVIVAL
G'DAY BLUE
NULLA CREEK
LAST THING TO LEARN
OLD TIME COUNTRY HALLS
SINGER FROM DOWN UNDER
BIBLE OF THE BUSH
REGAL ZONOPHONE
DROVIN'
CRYING ON EACH OTHER'S SHOULDER
THAT'S THE SONG WE'RE SINGING
JACK O'HAGAN
CHARLEVILLE
RINGER FROM THE TOP END
WHEN YOUR PANTS BEGIN TO GO
ME AND MATILDA
WHO WANTS MOSS?

91 OVER 50
BORN A TRAVELLING MAN
I HOPE THEY FIGHT AGAIN
A WORD TO TEXAS JACK
HOW WILL I GO WITH HIM, MATE?
MUST'VE BEEN A HELL OF A PARTY
GUMTREES BY THE ROADWAY
DO YOU THINK I DO NOT KNOW
NED KELLY WAS A GENTLEMAN
CATTLE CAMP CROONER
KELLY'S OFFSIDER
RINGER'S STOMP
DUNCAN
WHEN THE RAIN TUMBLES DOWN IN JULY
OLD TIME COUNTRY HALLS

MAKIN' A MILE
MY HEAVEN ON EARTH
RECYCLED RINGER
BOOMAROO FLYER

STAR TRUCKER
NAMES UPON THE WALL
THE LADY IS A TRUCKER
MECHANISED SWAGGIES
NO GOOD TRUCKIN' MAN
THE FLOOD OF '95
RINGERS RIGS & DRIVERS
BIG OLD MACK
DEAD ON TIME
HAULIN FOR THE DOUBLE 'T'
SOMETHING IN THE PILLIGA

THE VERY BEST OF SLIM DUSTY
A PUB WITH NO BEER
LIGHTS ON THE HILL
THE BIGGEST DISAPPOINTMENT
THREE RIVERS HOTEL
RINGER FROM THE TOP END
WHERE COUNTRY IS
LEAVE HIM IN THE LONG YARD
PLAINS OF PEPPIMENARTI
DUNCAN
CHARLEVILLE
INDIAN PACIFIC
SWEENY
G'DAY G'DAY
WALK A COUNTRY MILE
WHEN THE RAIN TUMBLES DOWN IN JULY
I'M GOING BACK AGAIN TO YARRAWONGA
OLD TIME COUNTRY HALLS
CAMOOWEAL
WE'VE DONE US PROUD
COUNTRY REVIVAL
CUNNAMULLA FELLER
BY THE FIRE OF GIDGEE COAL
LOSIN' MY BLUES TONIGHT
WOBBLY BOOT

'99
BINIEYE BALL
SWAGLESS SWAGGIE
ABALINGA MAIL
BANJO

IT'S GOOD TO SEE YOU MATE
DIGGIN' A HOLE
GHOST OF BEN HALL
KELLY'S COUNTRY KITCHEN
OUTBACK
NO BIDS FOR THE BAY
MUSTERING IN FULL SWING
BUSHMAN'S PRAYER .
ALONG THE ROAD TO NULLA NULLA

LOOKING FORWARD, LOOKING BACK
LOOKING FORWARD, LOOKING BACK
NEVER WAS AT ALL
THERE'S A RAINBOW OVER THE ROCK
MATILDA NO MORE
THE BLOKE WHO SERVES THE BEER
PADDY WILLIAM
CLEAN UP OUR OWN BACKYARD
OLD TIME COUNTRY SONGS
A BAD DAY'S FISHING
PORT AUGUSTA
GOOD HEAVENS ABOVE
HOOKS & RIDE
KEELA VALLEY COALS
MEMORIES AND DREAMS
LOOKING FORWARD, LOOKING BACK (REPRISE)

THE MAN WHO IS AUSTRALIA 5 CD SET
(NOTE DUPLICATE TRACKS ARE DIFFERENT RECORDINGS)
DISC 1 RAMBLIN' SHOES
HELLO AND GOODBYE
TRAVELLIN' THROUGH
I WANT A PARDON FOR DADDY
MOTHER
THE QUEEN OF HEARTS
EUMERELLA SHORES
MUSIC MY DAD PLAYED TO ME
HAPPY JACK
YOU TOOK THE JOY OUT OF LIVING
IF ONLY I HAD A HOME SWEET HOME
I'VE BEEN TALKING TO GRANNIE
MANY MOTHERS
MY SON

SWEET THANG
THE SUNSET YEARS OF LIFE
DEATH ROW
CAMOOWEAL
RAMBLIN' SHOES
JUST LOVIN' YOU
RIDIN' THE ROAD
I'VE BEEN THERE (AND BACK AGAIN)
DISC 2 RAMBLIN' SHOES VOLUME 2
DUNCAN
KILOMETRES ARE STILL MILES TO ME
WHERE I'D SOONER BE
LOGAN
TO WHOM IT MAY CONCERN
WHEN THE RAIN TUMBLES DOWN IN JULY
LARRIKINS LANDING
LIGHTS ON THE HILL
CHARLEVILLE
MAD JOE THE FISHERMAN
ANOTHER NIGHT IN BROOME
MORNING COMES EARLY
I NEED TO FIND A PLACE
MITCHELL GRASS
LEAVING ONLY DUST
DISC 3 FROM THE DUSTY TREASURE CHEST
THE PUB WITH NO BEER
RINGER FROM THE TOP END
LIGHTS ON THE HILL
NATURAL HIGH
CHARLEVILLE
QUICKSILVER
WHY WORRY NOW
TRUTHFUL FELLA
MY PAL ALCOHOL
BEEN A FOOL TOO LONG
WALTZING MATILDA
WHEN THE RAIN TUMBLES DOWN IN JULY
I'M GOING BACK AGAIN TO YARRAWONGA
NATURAL HIGH
SANTA'S GONNA COME IN A MAIL COACH
CHRISTMAS ON THE STATION
SANTA LOOKED A LOT LIKE DADDY (AND DADDY LOOKED A
LOT LIKE HIM)

THE PUB WITH NO BEER
WHEN THE RAIN TUMBLES DOWN IN JULY
DISC 4 LIVE IN CONCERT
INTRODUCTION AND SPACE SHUTTLE BROADCAST 1981
WALK A COUNTRY MILE
MIDDLETON'S ROUSEABOUT
DINKI DI AUSSIE
INDIAN PACIFIC
MEDLEY: I MUST HAVE GOOD TERBACCY WHEN
I SMOKE/ SWEENY/TRUMBY/THE BIGGEST DISAPPOINTMENT
SHE'LL BE RIGHT, MATE
HE'S A GOOD BLOKE WHEN HE'S SOBER, BUT
DUNCAN
CATTLEMEN FROM THE HIGH PLAINS
GLORY BOUND TRAIN
THE PUB WITH NO BEER
MY DAD WAS A ROADTRAIN MAN
CHARLEVILLE
LIGHTS ON THE HILL
WALK A COUNTRY MILE
ABALINGA MAIL
DISC 5 THE WAY I SEE IT (INTERVIEW DISC)
SLIM DUSTY IN CONVERSATION WITH NICK ERBY (NOT USED
IN STORY)

WEST OF WINTON
WALTZING MATILDA
WEST OF WINTON
SADDLE UP AND RIDE
THE VANISHING BREED
THE OLD SADDLE
TRUTHFUL FELLA
OLD SCOBIE
BACK WITH THE SHOW AGAIN
FINNEY'S HOME BREW
THE SHEARER'S STORY
OLD DINGO
HAPPY ANNIVERSARY
HAM AND EGGS
SASSAFRAS GAP
DAN THE WRECK

**THE MEN FROM THE NULLA NULLA – REUNITED AND
REVISITED**
THE MEN FROM THE NULLA NULLA
RIDING THROUGH THE VALLEY IN SPRING
FAR GRANDEST HOMESTEAD OF ALL
GOOD OLD DAYS
DRY WEATHER WIND
EASY GOIN' DRIFTER
WILLY WILLY
TEN GOLDEN RULES
OLD KENTUCKY RIG
SONG OF THE MACLEAY
THE OLD RUSTY BELL
ANSWER TO THE OLD RUSTY BELL
SOMEWHERE UP IN QUEENSLAND
JOY BELLS IN YOUR HEART
HEAVEN COUNTRY STYLE
MY OLD AUSSIE HOMESTEAD
BALLAD OF PORT MACQUARIE
SOMEBODY'S MOTHER
THE PAPER BOY
SOMEBODY'S MOTHER TONIGHT
ROSE OF RED RIVER
WINTER WINDS

**TRAVELLIN' STILL...ALWAYS WILL WITH ANNE
KIRKPATRICK**
END OF THE BITUMEN
TRAVELLIN' STILL, ALWAYS WILL
TRACKS I LEFT BEHIND
MAN ON THE SIDE OF THE ROAD
JUST AN OLD CATTLEDOG
BELT & BUCKLED
BONNER (THE QUIET ACHIEVER)
YOU AND MY OLD GUITAR
I WONDER IF THE CREEKS ARE STILL FLOWING
CLAYPAN BOOGIE
SUNDOWN
TAKING ON WHAT'S NEXT!
THE MEN WHO TRY AND TRY

SIDE BY SIDE (THE DUSTY COLLABORATIONS)
TWO SINGERS (ONE SONG)
THE BIGGEST DISAPPOINTMENT
A FIRE OF GIDGEE COAL
MATILDA NO MORE
WE'RE JUST A COUPLE OF BOYS FROM THE BUSH
WHEN THE RAIN TUMBLES DOWN IN JULY
LIGHTS ON THE HILL
WHEN THE CURRAWONGS COME DOWN
DUNCAN
SUNSET YEARS OF LIFE
COUNTRY REVIVAL
PUB WITH NO BEER
RIDING THROUGH THE VALLEY IN SPRING
CHRISTMAS, WHEN I WAS BIG AS YOU
I LOVE TO HAVE A DANCE WITH DOROTHY

COLUMBIA LANE THE LAST SESSIONS
BLUE HILLS IN THE DISTANCE
ROLLING DOWN THE ROAD
NATURE'S GENTLEMAN
ANSWER TO BILLY
LONG DISTANCE DRIVING
I'M GONNA TAKE MY DOG FOR A RUN
GET ALONG

THE VERY BEST OF SLIM DUSTY TRACKS
LOOKING FORWARD, LOOKING BACK
A PUB WITH NO BEER
LIGHTS ON THE HILL
THE BIGGEST DISAPPOINTMENT
THREE RIVERS HOTEL
RINGER FROM THE TOP END
WHERE COUNTRY IS
LEAVE HIM IN THE LONG YARD
PLAINS OF PEPPIMENARTI
DUNCAN
CHARLEVILLE
INDIAN PACIFIC
SWEENY (LIVE)
G'DAY G'DAY
WALK A COUNTRY MILE
WHEN THE RAIN TUMBLES DOWN IN JULY

I'M GOING BACK AGAIN TO YARRAWONGA (LIVE)
OLD TIME COUNTRY HALLS
CAMOOWEAL
WE'VE DONE US PROUD
COUNTRY REVIVAL
CUNNAMULLA FELLER
BY THE FIRE OF GIDGEE COAL
LOSIN' MY BLUES TONIGHT (LIVE)
WALTZING MATILDA

SLIM DUSTY LIVE
I'M GOING TO YARRAWONGA
THAT OLD BUSH SHANTY OF MINE (MEDLEY)
LEAVE HIM IN THE LONG YARD
INTRODUCTION
THE SADDLE IS HIS HOME (TALL DARK
MAN IN THE SADDLE)
I GOT YOU
WHERE COUNTRY IS
IF I NEEDED YOU
INDIAN PACIFIC
INTRODUCTION
NATURAL HIGH
LOOKING FORWARD LOOKING BACK
NEVER WAS AT ALL
ABALINGA MAIL
NAMES UPON THE WALL
NO GOOD TRUCKIN' MAN
INTRODUCTION
THE MAN FROM THE NEVER NEVER
THE SUNDLANDER (INSTRUMENTAL)
OUR WEDDING WALTZ
KELLY'S OFFSIDER
HILLS OF HOME
YODEL MEDLEY
A PUB WITH NO BEER
DUNCAN
MY OLD PAL
GOOD HEAVENS ABOVE
ALONG THE ROAD TO NULLA NULLA (INSTRUMENTAL)
BROWN BOTTLE BLUES
CLAYPAN BOOGIE
INTRODUCTION

LOSING MY BLUES TONIGHT
INTRODUCTION
LIGHTS ON THE HILL

AUSTRALIAN BUSH BALLADS & OLD TIME SONG TRACKS
WHEN THE RAIN TUMBLES DOWN IN JULY
ROPE & SADDLE BLUES
OLD ROCKING HORSE
DYING STOCKMAN
BILL
BLACK VELVET BAND
WORD TO TEXAS JACK
CATTLE CAMP REVERIE
WHOA, BULLOCKS, WHOA
BATTLE WITH THE ROAN
EUMERELLA SHORE
ITCHING FEET

SONGS FOR ROLLING STONES
BORN TO BE A ROLLING STONE
ROVIN' GAMBLER
BUMMING AROUND
WHISKEY BLUES
MAY I SLEEP IN YOUR BARN TONIGHT, MISTER
ROAD TO GUNDAGAI
THREE TIMES SEVEN
LITTLE BLOSSOM
TRAVELLIN' GUITAR
DOWN THE TRACK
I'LL BE A BACHELOR TILL I DIE
SOMEBODY'S MOTHER TONIGHT

SLIM DUSTY SINGS
SUNLANDER
MOTHER
RAIN STILL TUMBLES DOWN IN JULY
LONESOME ROAD OF TEARS
KING BUNDAWAAL
SINCE THE BUSHLAND BOOGIE CAME THIS WAY
HARRY THE BREAKER
WALKIN' ON MY WAY
LITTLE GIRL DRESSED IN BLUE
NATURE OF MAN

GUMTREES BY THE ROADWAY
ROARING WHEELS

REUNION
HOW GOOD IT IS – SLIM DUSTY
ROAD DREAMIN' - ANNE KIRKPATRICK
RESTING PLACE – JAMES ARNEMAN, HANNAH KIRKPATRICK
OLD PURPLE – DAVE KIRKPATRICK
TOOK HIS SADDLE HOME – ANNE KIRKPATRICK
PICK IT UP AND PASS IT ON – JAMES ARNEMAN, SLIM DUSTY
FAMILY, ANNE KIRKPATRICK, DAVE KIRKPATRICK
TOO MANY MEMORIES (TO FORGET) – JOY McKEAN
SUNBURNT PEOPLE – SLIM DUSTY
KEEP ON ROLLING (THE SONG) – DAVID KIRKPATRICK
HIGH, WIDE AND HANDSOME – KATE ARNEMAN
DREAMER – HANNAH KIRKPATRICK
MIDDLE OF THE ROAD - JAMES ARNEMAN
FAMILY REUNION – SLIM DUSTY FAMILY, JOY McKEAN
FROM THERE TO NOW – ANNE KIRKPATRICK
SLIM DUSTY RECORDING – SLIM DUSTY (DVD) (*) NOT USED
IN STORY

TRAVELLIN' STILL/ COLUMBIA LANE
BORN A TRAVELLIN' MAN – SLIM DUSTY, URBAN, KEITH
I HOPE THEY FIGHT AGAIN – SLIM DUSTY, COSTER, STAN
A WORD TO TEXAS JACK – SLIM DUSTY, DUSTY, SLIM
HOW WILL I GO WITH HIM, MATE? – SLIM DUSTY,
CORMACK, MACK
MUST'VE BENN A HELL OF A PARTY – SLIM DUSTY,
DUSTY, SLIM
GUM TREES BY THE ROADWAY – SLIM DUSTY, DUSTY, SLIM
DO YOU THINK THAT I DO NOT KNOW – SLIM DUSTY,
DUSTY, SLIM
NED KELLY WAS A GENTLEMAN – SLIM DUSTY, DUSTY, SLIM
CATTLECAMP CROONER – SLIM DUSTY, DUSTY, SLIM
RINGER'S STOMP – SLIM DUSTY, DUSTY, SLIM
DUNCAN – SLIM DUSTY, ALEXANDER, PAT
KELLY'S OFFSIDER – SLIM DUSTY, McKEAN, JOY
WHEN THE RAIN TUMBLES DOWN IN JULY – SLIM DUSTY,
DUSTY, SLIM
OLD TIME COUNTRY HALLS – SLIM DUSTY, DUSTY, SLIM
BLUE HILLS (IN THE DISTANCE) – SLIM DUSTY,
DOHLING, JOHN

111

ROLLING DOWN THE ROAD – SLIM DUSTY, COOK, CHRIS
NATURE'S GENTLEMAN – SLIM DUSTY, BLUNDEL, JAMES
ANSWER TO BILLY – SLIM DUSTY, DOHLING, JOHN
LONG DISTANCE DRIVING – SLIM DUSTY, FENDER, ACE
GONNA TAKE MY DOG FOR A RUN – SLIM DUSTY, BLAKE,
KENNY JOE
GET ALONG – SLIM DUSTY, WALKER, DON

BIBLIOGRAPHY

THE FOLLOWING ALBUMS WERE FOUND AT
http://www.slimdusty.com.au/discography.html
AUSSIE SING SONG
SONGS IN THE SADDLE
ANOTHER AUSSIE SING SONG
PEOPLE AND PLACES
THE NATURE OF MAN
AN EVENING WITH SLIM AND JOY
ESSENTIALLY AUSTRALIAN
SONGS MY FATHER SANG TO ME
SONGS FROM THE CATTLE CAMPS
SING ALONG WITH DAD
CATTLE CAMP CROONER
SLIM DUSTY ENCORES
SING A HAPPY SONG
SONGS FROM THE LAND I LOVE
GLORY BOUND TRAIN
LIVE AT WAGGA WAGGA
ME AND MY GUITAR
FOOLIN' AROUND
LIVE AT TAMWORTH
DUSTY TRACKS
TALL STORIES AND SAD SONGS AUSTRALIANA
DINKI DI AUSSIES
LIGHTS ON THE HILL
WAY OUT THERE
THINGS I SEE AROUND ME
GIVE ME THE ROAD
SONGS FROM DOWN UNDER
JUST SLIM WITH OLD FRIENDS
ON THE MOVE
TRAVELLIN' COUNTRY MAN
TO WHOM IT MAY CONCERN
THE ENTERTAINER
SPIRIT OF AUSTRALIA
RARITIES
RODEO RIDERS
WALK COUNTRY MILE
THE SLIM DUSTY FAMILY ALBUM
THE MAN WHO STEADIES THE LEAD
NO 50 GOLDEN ANNIVERSARY

WHO'S RIDING OLD HARLEQUIN NOW?
WHERE IS COUNTRY
ON THE WALLABY
I HAVEN'T CHANGED A BIT
TRUCKS ON THE TRACK
THE SLIM DUSTY MOVIE
I'LL TAKE MINE COUNTRY STYLE
SINGER FROM DOWN UNDER
TO A MATE – SLIM DUSTY REMEMBERS "MACK"
CORMACK
BEER DRINKING SONGS OF AUSTRALIA
AUSTRALIA IS HIS NAME
"LIVE" ACROSS AUSTRALIA (THE SLIM DUSTY
FAMILY)
STORIES I WANTED TO TELL
COUNTRY LIVIN'
CATTLEMEN FROM THE HIGH PLAINS
HERITAGE ALBUM
SLIM DUSTY SINGS STAN COSTER
NEON CITY
G'DAY G'DAY
KING OF KALGOORLIE
HENRY LAWSON AND BANJO PATERSON
TWO SINGERS ONE SONG
A LAND HE CALLS HIS OWN
COMING HOME
SLIM DUSTY SINGS JOY McKEAN
TRAVELLIN' GUITAR
THAT'S THE SONG WE'RE SINGING
LIVE INTO THE 90s
THE ANNIVERSARY ALBUM NO. 2
RINGER FROM THE TOP END
REGAL ZONOPHONE COLLECTION
NATURAL HIGH
COUNTRY WAY OF LIFE
FIDDLER MAN
THE SLIM DUSTY SHOW – LIVE IN TOWNSVILLE 1956
COUNTRY CLASSICS – SLIM DUSTY
91 OVER 50
THE VERY BEST OF SLIM DUSTY
MAKIN' A MILE
LOOKING FORWARD, LOOKING BACK
'99

THE MAN WHO IS AUSTRALIA
WEST OF WINTON
THE MEN FROM NULLA NULLA – REUNITED AND
REVISITED
TRAVELLIN' STILL… ALWAYS WILL WITH ANNE
KIRKPATRICK
SIDE BY SIDE (THE DUSTY COLLABORATIONS)
COLUMBIA LANE THE LAST SESSIONS

The Very Best Of Slim Dusty:http://www.music-city.org/Slim-Dusty/The-Very-Best-of-Slim-Dusty-32463/

Slim Dusty Live: http://www.music-city.org/Slim-Dusty/ Slim-Dusty-Live-687369/

Australian Bush Ballads & Old Time Songs:http://www.music-city.org/Slim-Dusty/Australian-Bush-Ballads_AND-Old-Time-Son...

Songs For Rolling Stones:http://www.music-city.org/Slim-Dusty/Songs-for-Rolling-Stones-375368/

Slim Dusty Sings: http://www.music-city.org/Slim-Dusty/ Slim-Dusty-Sings-375260/

Reunion: http://www.music-city.org/Slim-Dusty/Reunion-825422/

Travellin Still/Columbia Lane:http://www.music-city.org/Slim-Dusty/Travellin-StillColumbia-Lane-757564/

ABOUT THE AUTHOR

I was 59 years old; a mother of three very special and supportive children and a grandmother of three wonderful grandsons (I now have five grand-children.) when I started writing my first book whilst watching a Bon Jovi concert DVD. (I am an avid fan, if you can call me that; crazy is more like it.)

I write from the heart and I really enjoyed writing the book, so I wrote another using a different artist, and the books kept coming to me and I kept writing them.(with a little help from above.)

Because I use different artist/artists song titles I have to be very careful with Copyright so a lot of legal requirements have to be taken into consideration before publishing the books. I also needed a name that would connect my books to each other; so the "Song Title Series" books began.

All my books are short stories; however it depends on how many song titles there are to be used, as to the length of the book. Some artists didn't have enough song titles on their own so I combined them with a few other artists. Other artists had that many song titles that I could have written a novel; but it would have ended up being boring.

Challenges I like, so writing books with various artists are a lot of fun and need careful thinking.

Why should I have all the fun writing the books and not be able to share them with everyone; so I have converted them into large print books so that you can share my fun as well.

Hopefully in the not too distant future; the books will also be available as audio books so that no-one will miss out on my fun and enjoyment of writing these unique books. I hope that you enjoy reading them.

My web site www.songtitleseries.com is the place to visit for updates of new books and the place to purchase other titles in all formats.

TESTIMONIALS

After reading through your range of books I felt I must compliment you Joan on the imaginative and entertaining way in which you presented each group and the Musicians in those groups. The way the stories were constructed is a credit to your work ethic. These must have taken considerable time to piece together and it is obviously a work of love for you.
I wish you all the success you truly deserve and look forward to seeing you next time you visit Tamworth.
Peter Harkins
Managing Director Cheapa Music
Country Music Capital Tamworth

Joan has come up with a really unique concept with this 'Song Title Series" I found this book interesting, and was fascinated at the way she has included so many song titles into the story. It's a great read and something a little different from most novels.
Adam Harvey (Australian Country Music Artist)

"Having read three of the Song Title Series, all in the Country Music field, I found them to be a very interesting and refreshing change to the usual books that I read. Joan has written them very well, and has used loads of imagination and cleverness to make them very unique! Very impressive!!"
Colleen B.
Tamworth (Country Music Capital)

Joan Maguire Books are very nice, I enjoy reading them so much, they are hard to put down!! Especially when she does one about Bonjovi and their songs!!!If I can say, it is worth every penny, when you buy one!!! The Books make nice presents, for a person whom loves to read!!!
I can guarantee that you will LOVE these books, because I do!!!!!!!!!
Dawn from Newark, Delaware in the United States of America

I am Susie and would like to tell you guys, how much I am enjoying Joan Maguire's Books!! They are very enjoyable, and they are something that you do not ever want to put down!! I really enjoy these books; I can't wait until the next one that she puts out!!!!!!! I say go to your local book store, today and get one, you will not be disappointed!!!!!
Sue-from the United States of America

The song titles series are books that were intriguing and were hard to believe that these short stories were written within the incorporated song titles of the artists that are mentioned in the titles. I loved what I have read so far and think that anyone with an imagination and love of music as the author you will surely enjoy reading these.
L.K. Brisbane Australia.